Logizomai

Logizomai

A Reasonable Faith in an Unreasonable World

KYLE MCDANELL

RESOURCE *Publications* • Eugene, Oregon

LOGIZOMAI
A Reasonable Faith in an Unreasonable World

Copyright © 2011 Kyle McDanell. All rights reserved. Except for brief quotations in critical publications or reviews, no part of this book may be reproduced in any manner without prior written permission from the publisher. Write: Permissions, Wipf and Stock Publishers, 199 W. 8th Ave., Suite 3, Eugene, OR 97401.

Resource Publications
An Imprint of Wipf and Stock Publishers
199 W. 8th Ave., Suite 3
Eugene, OR 97401
www.wipfandstock.com

ISBN 13: 978-1-60899-482-3

Manufactured in the U.S.A.

"Scripture quotations taken from the New American Standard Bible , Copyright 1960, 1962, 1963, 1968, 1971, 1972, 1973, 1975, 1977, 1995 by The Lockman Foundation Used by Permission." (www.Lockman.org)

To my young son Elijah who is the future of our family, nation, and faith. May he be bold in the gospel, faithful to the cross, and articulate in the Spirit in a world that will be more depraved in his day than it already is in mine.

1 Timothy 1:15–20

"As I urged you upon my departure for Macedonia, remain on at Ephesus so that you may instruct certain men not to teach strange doctrines, nor to pay attention to myths and endless genealogies, which give rise to mere speculation rather than furthering the administration of God which is by faith. But the goal of our instruction is love from a pure heart and a good conscience and a sincere faith. For some men, straying from these things, have turned aside to fruitless discussion, wanting to be teachers of the Law, even though they do not understand either what they are saying or the matters about which they make confident assertion. But we know that the Law is good, if one uses it lawfully, realizing the fact that law is not made for a righteous person, but for those who are lawless and rebellious, for the ungodly and sinners, for the unholy and profane, for those who kill their fathers or mothers, for murderers and immoral men and homosexuals and kidnappers and liars and perjurers, and whatever else is contrary to sound teaching, according to the glorious gospel of the blessed God, with which I have been entrusted. I thank Christ Jesus our Lord, who has strengthened me, because He considered me faithful, putting me into service, even though I was formerly a blasphemer and a persecutor and a violent aggressor yet I was shown mercy because I acted ignorantly in unbelief; and the grace of our Lord was more than abundant, with the faith and love which are found in Christ Jesus. It is a trustworthy statement deserving full acceptance that Christ Jesus came into the world to save sinners, among whom I am foremost of all. Yet for this reason I found mercy, so that in me as the foremost, Jesus Christ might demonstrate His perfect patience as an example for those who would believe in Him for eternal life. Now to the King eternal, immortal, invisible, the only God, be honor and glory forever and ever. Amen. This command I entrust to you, Timothy, my son, in accordance with the prophecies previously made concerning you, that by them you fight the good fight, keeping faith and a good conscience, which some have rejected and suffered shipwreck in regard to their faith."

1 Timothy 1:3–19

Contents

Foreword xi
Preface xiii
Acknowledgment xv
Introduction xvii

PART ONE THEOLOGY: WHERE REASONABLE FAITH MEETS UNREASONABLE BELIEFS

1. We Are All Theologians 3
   The Root of Everything We Are and Do

2. Credo, We Believe in Something 7
   National Council of Churches Release a New Creed

3. Twice the Son of Hell 11
   An Atheist Visits Lakewood

4. Accommodationism Breeds Irrelevancy 17
   Why Liberalism Fails and the Transcendent Gospel Triumphs

5. Freud's Wish Fulfillment 24
   Why Atheism Can't Explain Atheism

6. Piñata Theology 28
   Ignore the Issue and Swing at the Distraction— What Piper has Taught Us About the Church

7. "Friendship With the World Is Enmity With God" 32
   Rick Warren Tries to Have It Both Ways

8. Have We Forgotten the Gospel? 36
   Glenn Beck, Social Justice, and the Gospel of Jesus Christ

Part Two Culture: Where Reasonable Faith Meets Unreasonable Society

9. The Utopian Myth 43
   Pandora and Avatar Blues

10. The Missing Story 49
    Ida and the Search for Secular Validation

11. The Personhood of Animals 52
    The Argument Is Made . . . Again

12. Married with Children . . . Lots of Them! 60

13. Abortion 64
    Is Common Ground Possible?

14. The Anti-Choice Sinner and the Abortionist Saint 71
    One a Martyr, the Other a Nuisance

15. Where Does the Madness End? 75
    The Dire Destination of the Homosexual Agenda—Part 1

16. Where Does the Madness End? 78
    Where the Homosexual Agenda Leads—Part 2

17. Punishing Prejudice by Being Prejudice 85
    The Lesson and Legacy of Hate Crimes

18. The Missing Gene 89
    The Failed Search for the Gay Gene

19. The Next Step 94
    Is Polyamory the Next Sexual Movement?

PART THREE   POLITICS: WHERE REASONABLE FAITH MEETS UNREASONABLE POLICY

20   Must Conservatives Believe in God? 99
     The Role of God in Shaping Our Politics

21   The Lion of the Senate Meets the Lamb of God 107
     The Pope, the Politician, and the Plea for Grace

22   The Transcendence of Greed 111
     What Economics Can Teach Us About the Gospel

23   What Is to Be Our Response 114
     Living as a Christian in an Obama Administration

24   Prophet, Priest, and President 121
     Is Obama Really the Messiah?

25   The Real Solution to Global Warming 125
     Human Extinction

Conclusion 131
Bibliography 137

Foreword

IN HIS debut work, Kyle McDanell has produced a unique work that calls evangelical believers to a life and a worldview that resembles the Author of their salvation. McDanell's book will challenge believers to engage in an honest conversation with themselves about the importance of connecting a lost and dying culture with the gospel. This call to an authentic Christian life confronts lukewarm believers in a way that many believers long for – the love of a competent and protective Shepherd who will point toward the authority of the Scriptures in all things pertaining to justification and sanctification. McDanell, a well respected pastor who is mighty in the Scriptures, gives his audience a clear call to an understanding of those issues that pervade society and that touch many in a personal way. McDanell applies a reasonable faith to all dimensions of life whether it be against unorthodox theologies, societal decay, or depraved policies or in favor of sound doctrine or gospel-driven convictions and truths—all of which the author is clearly passionate.

The tenor of this book will convict and move the reader to uphold the faith once for all handed down to the saints (Jude 3). This important work will set the theological engagement pace in which the author, time and time again, points us towards the Savior, Jesus Christ.

Nicholas Clark
Pastor, Cash Creek Baptist Church
Henderson, KY

Preface

As a pastor, I understand what it means to be frustrated and broken hearted. I oftentimes find myself in broken homes, comforting mourning families, and picking up the pieces that open, unrepentant sin leaves behind. It is easy to give up and call it quits. The world is a mess and the lives of most Christians do not look much better. Call it ignorance. Call it indifference. Call it cowardice. Call it bad theology. Regardless of the name, Christians simply do not seem to understand nor do we live by the gospel of Christ.

I believe that the only hope the Church has is the gospel of Jesus Christ. His death and resurrection accompanied with our belief and repentance is the only hope and the only foundation by which to stand on. The gospel has been cheapened in our pulpits, ignored in our homes, and silenced in our culture. Every day is a reminder of how the gospel should shape all that we say, do, think, act, confess, and believe.

The gospel shapes our worldview, our voting habits, our conversations, our faith, our worship, our evangelism, our families, our relationships, and our understanding of the world and humanity. I am convinced that what we need more than anything is a return to the gospel. We cannot have a revival or a spiritual awakening or be able to articulate our faith without a return to the gospel.

This book is about the gospel and how it shapes our thinking. Christians are under assault from the culture to abandon their faith and convictions. Because the gospel has been ignored by so many of our brothers and sisters in Christ, we have become all too willing to give in to the pressures of the depraved world around us.

My goal in this book is to show the reader how the gospel is more than just words on a page, a simple prayer without regenera-

Preface

tion, or a philosophy to adapt, but a lifestyle to be embraced and a worldview to be articulated. Our hope and faith is shaped by the message of the gospel and it is our responsibility as Christians, to articulate it without apology. Until Christians understand and apply the gospel in our world today, we will be fools to believe that somehow the culture will be "redeemed."

I pray that the reader will be awaken from their spiritual slumber and ready to engage the culture, evangelize the lost, and embrace the saving gospel of Jesus Christ.

Acknowledgment

THERE ARE so many people to thank who have contributed in their own way to the publishing of this book. Without a doubt, if it were not for the grace of God, this book would have never been accomplished. God, in His goodness, has redeemed me though I did not deserved or earn it. It would be foolish for me to assume that my own wit or abilities has granted me this opportunity. As God has granted me grace, he continues to grant me unmerited blessings. He deserves greater worship than we could ever offer Him in a million lifetimes.

I must also thank my wife for her patience and encouragement for this entire process. Through long, late nights and stress, she has only encouraged me throughout this endeavor as a faithful, loving wife. Proverbs 31:10 asks who can find "an excellent wife?" I have found one and "her worth is far above jewels."

I must also thank the church I have been blessed to serve: Goshen Baptist Church. For over two hundred years, God has used this rural community to spread the gospel and He continues that work today. I pray that this book only adds to the legacy of faithfully proclaiming the gospel that Goshen has obediently sought to fulfill. God is not done with us yet.

Furthermore, I must thank everyone who has helped throughout the editing process including the publisher, the Adkins', and numerous others who have given me insight and correction along the way. I have benefitted from the wisdom of many saints and professionals.

Finally, I must mention the countless number of friends and family members who have in some measure contributed to this effort. Your patience and encouragement have made this possible. May God continue to use you in my life and in the lives of His saints.

Introduction

ATTEND ANY typical church in America and you will see a sad sight. Apathy. Division. Hypocrisy. Pride. Anger. Frustrations. Complaining. Factions. And rampant sin. Why? I believe it is because Christians are ignorant of the gospel. We have bought into cheap grace, a discounted devotion that fails in its sincerity and ignores the will of God.

No wonder the world mocks Christians. Ask the average church member what the gospel is, why marriage is so central to the Christian and to society, why the world is in such dire straits, and what it means to be a Christian and the ignorance of Christians will be evident. Most Christians in America today are spiritually stupid and culturally corrupted. No wonder. Scripture means little to the average believer. Sure, we hold our Bibles up high . . . only to place it on a shelf, until next Sunday. We spend more time chasing fads, updating our music ministry, playing the latest messy game with our youth, telling the latest jokes in our pulpits, and complaining about the future in our senior adult ministry than we seek doctrinal fidelity, proclaiming the gospel, and evangelizing the lost. The average church could not care less about the gospel, the Christian worldview, or even what it means to be a Christian. Thus, we have become a body of ignorant, short-sighted, inadequate believers who show up on Sunday to be entertained. As a result, most Christians fail to be challenged, exhorted, or called to reach a world that is hurting and longing for answers in which we are to be prepared to give and yet are all too often too lazy to provide.

The Church is in awful shape! The world walks by and we have nothing to say. Rather than engage our culture with the truths of the gospel, Scripture, sound theology, and the Christian world-

Introduction

view, we passively ignore the realities around us. People are hurting. Families are splitting. Men are growing up not knowing what it means to be a man, a husband, or a father. The sad state of our churches are reflected in the sad state of our marriages, home lives, relationships with the lost, and dysfunctional churches.

What Christians need most is the gospel. Where we turn for such a message is Scripture. Scripture not only shapes our understanding of God, but it also establishes our worldview. If we really believe in the Bible as the ultimate and exclusive source of truth, then we should let it shape what we believe, how we act, how we interact, what we say, and how we engage the culture.

By the looks of things, we Christians honor Jesus with our lips, but dishonor Him with our ignorance, apathy, and unconcern for the hurting, lost world around us. Our hearts are revealed, not in the checks we put in the offering plate for other church members to see, but in how little we care about the dying world around us. We pray more for the size of our wallets than for our responsibilities as ambassadors for Christ.

God save us from our apathetic cowardice!

So what is real Christianity? In our world today, there are extremes. First, there is the "fire insurance" faith that teaches that once we walk the aisle, say a prayer, and get baptized, we are "saved;" saved from the wrath of God; saved from hell; saved for eternity. It is true that the gospel is about one's standing before God and we must not under-emphasize that. However it is much more than just a free-ticket-out-of-hell card. A fire insurance faith cheapens the gospel because it does not address true repentance or obedience that God demands from all believers.

Secondly, others see the gospel as a social movement that seeks to abolish poverty, shelter the homeless, aid the sick and bring an end to war, violence, prejudice, and global warming. Christianity is not what we believe, they suggest, but what we do. Orthopraxy, not just orthodoxy. Right living, not just right belief.

Such a pseudo-gospel undermines right doctrine especially the substitutionary nature of the cross.

Though these two views are popular, neither option of what is real Christianity fully answers the question. Christianity is a worldview shaped by and centered around the gospel. It begins with our sinful standing before God, deserving wrath and hell, and yet on account of Christ, we have been forgiven and adopted as sons of God and heirs of Christ. That standing affects the believer's everyday life. Christians are to love as Christ loved us on the cross. We serve because Christ served us. We live selflessly because Christ did so on the cross. Out of that selflessness we must help the poor, the needy, the oppressed, the refugee, and the abused because only Christ can fix what is broken, heal what is sick, and make right all wrong. He is able to do this not because He's a great moral teacher, but because He is the Lord and Savior of all creation.

Christianity is a gospel-centered worldview. It begins with God and then moves to His Sovereign act of creation which became challenged by the willful rebellion of His image-bearers. After centuries of man seeking in vain to right his wrong against holy God by keeping the law and doing good works, God Himself, in human flesh, did what man could not. He saved us by reconciling us with our Maker. This salvation moves beyond a prayer and immediately proceeds into the world. Followers of Christ are to take the revelation of God and call men everywhere to repent. This command involves evangelism, righteous living, apologetics, service, and a complete worldview that reveals that all of man's hurts, struggles, and pains are remedied by the gospel of Jesus Christ.

The goal of this book is to define Christianity according to Scripture and outline how Christianity can be practically lived in obedience. Christianity is theological and all theology is practical. There is no such thing as a passive theology. Christianity engages the culture with the gospel. This book seeks to help the reader understand how the gospel shapes the Christian's worldview and how that worldview affects how one interacts and engages the culture.

Introduction

We will begin by looking at a number of theological and philosophical issues. A right theology is necessary for a right worldview. From a right worldview, one is able to address specific issues within the culture: abortion, sanctity of life, marriage, sex, family, homosexuality, and "political" issues. Though many Christians dangerously carry the flag higher than the cross, it remains necessary to see how the Christian worldview affects issues related to the political realm. Though Christians are accused of trying to legislate morality, Christianity's concern for the unborn, the definition of marriage, and the future of our nation is no different than the concerns of the secular left who fight with the same passion against their Christian counterparts.

A gospel-centered worldview engages life's many issues. The culture wars, the divisions, the arguments, and the debates are rooted in what people believe about God, creation, human depravity, and redemption. This book is a humble attempt to help Christians understand their worldview and what it looks like in our postmodern, secular culture. Rooted in Scripture and shaped by the gospel, I seek to engage, without fear, the culture in hopes of helping many make sense of the gospel and to further the kingdom of God to His glory and honor.

Part One

Theology: Where Reasonable Faith
Meets Unreasonable Beliefs

1

We Are All Theologians

The Root of Everything We Are and Do

ALL OF us are theologians. Whether one is an environmentalists greening his home or a scientists looking through his microscope looking for answers, everyone is a theologian. Every belief, every moral, every worldview, every conviction, every action, every spoken word, and every thought is based on one's theology. Everyone is a theologian.

Theology, and what it says about God, is the essence of every worldview. When we speak of worldviews, we are really dealing with theology. All of the cultural wars, political debates, disagreements, convictions, opinions, and shouting matches are the outworkings of a theology. Though most refuse to call it that, it is theology nonetheless.

With practical implications, theology answers tough questions like: Who is God? Where did we come from? What is wrong with this world? Why is there so much evil and suffering? What is the solution to this problem? What will the end of this world be like? How will it come about? What happens when we die? And yet to most today, theology is not practical. To them, it is an academic exercise whereby a group of people sit in an ivory tower and debate ancient documents that have no relevancy for today. Such a practice, however is not theology.

For example, a man lobbies his local Congressman to support a bill that would ban the spanking of children even by their parents out of the conviction that spanking is abusive and wrong. From where does such a conviction come? Most Americans were spanked at some point in their lives, and yet our hypothetical friend is against the practice and is fighting to ban it. Does his conviction come from Dr. Phil, watching too much Nanny 911, reading a popular parenting magazine or book, or from his own experience as a child and parent? No. This conviction is the result of his personal theological beliefs. He is a theologian. Our anti-spanking theologian believes that no child under any circumstance should be spanked.

The anti-spanking lobbyists is living out his theology. His conviction is likely rooted in his belief about human nature and the responsibilities of parents (anthropology), the affirmation in the existence of right and wrong, thus to do wrong is to sin (harmitology), and from his convictions about the character of God (theology).

Anthropology deals with man's nature. Is man inherently good or evil? More than likely, the spanking protestor likely believes that everyone is born inherently good, and thus the purpose of discipline should not be to break our evil nature, but to encourage and direct the good that is already present. Spanking, he might say, teaches the child to hit and to use violence as a tool to get what they want. Therefore, physical discipline will turn the innocent child into an abusive adult.

On the other hand, a pro-spanking defender might argue that children are not born purely innocent. They have selfish motives that manifest themselves early. Therefore, the goal of discipline is to establish order and to break the inherent selfishness already present from birth. Not to discipline, then, would only encourage the selfish nature thus leading to a more depraved individual.

The debate over human nature, showing itself in the debate over how to administer discipline, is called anthropology and has divided liberals and conservatives for centuries. Liberals traditionally affirm the goodness of human nature whereas most conservatives affirm the depravity of human nature. One's view about human nature shapes one's view of politics, economics, parenting, judicial theory, foreign policy, justice, and charity.

Furthermore, the spanking protestor clearly believes that to strike anyone, especially a child, for any reason, is inappropriate and thus should be stopped. Such a belief in right and wrong is centered on the theological issue of harmitology, or the doctrine of sin. Harmitology deals with what is right and wrong, sinful and righteous.

Finally, right and wrong must originate with God.[1] If there is a God, then there must be a right and wrong, and He determines what is righteous and sinful. God, the lobbyists likely believes, is a God of love. He cannot be vindictive and abusive. Therefore, to strike a child, even in the name of discipline, must surely run contrary to His nature and character. Though misguided, this is the work of theology.

Everyone is a theologian, whether one wants to acknowledge it or not. This implies three things. First, theology is central to truth. It is pointless to debate issues like marriage, war, poverty, global warming, government policies, and politicians without an understanding of the underlying theological convictions. To put theology on a shelf as if it does not matter is utter nonsense. Theology is always the root that determines our convictions and decision making, even if one is unaware that it is shaping those decisions.

This leads to the second point: theology is always relevant. Everything in life is a reflection of our theological assumptions and

1. This does not mean that atheist are amoral, but rather the atheist has no logical reason for their morality. If there is no God then everything is permissible. Morality runs contrary to evolution and the many attempts to provide naturalistic explanations for morality have failed miserably. Since we are moral beings, there must be a Divine Lawgiver. The universal existence of right and wrong is one of the most powerful arguments for the existence of God.

convictions. I am pro-life because of my convictions about God (theology) who created (creation) us in His image (anthropology). I believe that the solution to the problems of the world (soteriology) are not found in politics, policy, environmental activism, sexual liberation, social reformation, or national diplomacy, but in the gospel of Jesus Christ. Such a worldview is theological as are all worldviews. Theology is relevant as it shapes all of our worldviews which shapes how we vote, the decisions we make, the lives we live, and how we raise our children.

Thirdly, theology is practical. Oftentimes when a pastor presents theology a collective yawn proceeds from his congregation. Such a response is typical of our culture today. We all want answers, but by ignoring theology we are placing band-aids on our disease rather than curing our ills. The problem is not self-esteem, but sin. The problem is not the need to communicate, but to reconcile. The answer is not therapy, but repentance. So long as we treat the symptoms, we will never be cured of our disease. However, once we embrace the practicality of theology, real solutions to real problems can be implemented.

Theology is more than an academic exercise for those with many degrees. Theology is what everyone does everyday whether at the grocery store or at the abortion clinic. Everybody is a theologian and everybody has a theology. The question, then, is not *if* we have a theology, but whether or not it is the *right* theology. The burden of theology is not just what it says about us and our convictions, but about what it says concerning God and His character.

2

Credo, We Believe in Something

National Council of Churches Release a New Creed

WHAT DOES a Christian organization bent on unity over uniformity look like? The National Council of Churches (NCC) new creed shows us. The NCC is built on unifying various religious traditions in order to solve the issues of our day. The problem is that the council has compromised on all essential Christian doctrine. In search for unity, divisive doctrines like the full deity of Christ, the clarity and inspiration of Scripture, and substitutionary atonement are put aside and even denied.

As the years wear on, the NCC continues to sink deeper into theological liberalism. All that is left, once the cross is stripped of its glory and God is stripped of His revelation, is nothing more than a worldview bent on improving this world without a care for God's truth and the life to come. As C. S. Lewis argued, without the hope and focus on life after death, one has no motivation to change his life and world before death.[1]

---

1. Lewis wrote, "Hope is one of the Theological virtues. This means that a continual looking forward to the eternal world is not (as some modern people think) a form of escapism or wishful thinking, but one of the things a Christian is meant to do. It does not mean that we are to leave the present world as it is. If you read history you will find that the Christians who did most for the present world were just those who thought most of the next.... It is since Christians have largely ceased to think of the other world that they have become so ineffective in this. Aim at Heaven and you will get earth 'thrown in': aim at earth and you will

In 2007, the NCC adopted their Social Creed for the 21st Century that clearly reveals the council's focus and direction. As typical of ecumenical liberalism, the NCC is moving away from orthodoxy to a theology of humanitarian aide. The social gospel has replaced the theology of the cross. The 2007 document begins with the statement:

> Remembering the prophetic Social Creed of the Churches of 1908, we respond to God's call to transform our social order towards justice and peace, and address the 21st century's great challenges of globalization and sustainability. Hearing also concerns of churches and peoples around our globe, we pledge ourselves to specific practices of personal and social responsibility that reflect our Triune God's gracious will for all creation. We rejoice in the Biblical vision where all "shall long enjoy the work of their hands" and "not labor in vain or bear children for calamity" (Isa. 65:22–23).[2]

The creed goes on to list specific issues they seek to remedy like "employment for all," a fair justice system, the abolition of forced and child-labor, the "abatement of poverty," universal healthcare, and "redirection of military spending to more peaceful and productive uses."[3]

The creed itself is full of fallacies. Littered with political ideology, the NCC is clearly mixing religion and politics. Their concern for paid time off for all workers, universal healthcare, and affordable housing for all are classic examples of welding faith and politics. What is most telling, however, is not just in what the document says, but in what it fails to say. Mainly, there is no mention of the gospel. Nowhere in this creed is the foundation of the Christian faith stated or even hinted at. A Christian creed without the truth of the cross and resurrection which demands both belief and repentance is rather bleak. To strip any confession of this uncompromising doctrine is to cease to be Christian.

---

get neither" in Lewis, *Mere Christianity*, 134.
2. "A Social Creed for the 21st Century," lines 1–7.
3. Ibid., lines 43.

Credo, We Believe in Something

When the gospel is not clearly outlined and explained, even in a document that is set to outline goals of social policy and change, then all that is left is a progressive political ideology. With over twenty social items on the list (most of them political), the Council says nothing regarding abortion, the sanctity of life, bioethics, or the protection of marriage. They say much about equal rights for all, but apparently have no intentions on defending the rights of the unborn from abortion clinics or embryonic stem cell research.

Sometimes seeking the unity of the Church is worse than seeking truth via uniformity to the gospel, especially when politics trumps the gospel. By seeking unity rather than uniformity, one is forced to abandon all difficult doctrines as laid out in Scripture and the gospel. This creed is a reflection of the unorthodox social gospel within the NCC which replaces the gospel with politics and social reform. The goal then is no longer to save souls but to save the earth.

This move away from orthodoxy is inevitable. The NCC has followed the path of other organizations like it (such as the World Council of Churches). When uniformity to right doctrine is set aside, all that is left is humanitarian aide and progressive political agendas. The issues laid out in this document are well worth our time and effort to eradicate, but to resolve temporal problems at the cost of eternal realities runs contrary to the real message of Jesus. Jesus calls men everywhere to repent, not to pick up litter. Jesus did feed the hungry but only to point them to Himself; the Bread of Life.

The problem with this creed goes beyond politics; it undermines the gospel. Rather than pleading for man to run to Christ (the one who died so that in the end we would not have too), the NCC foolishly seeks temporal redemption in the depraved souls of men and their corrupt public policy. To replace the gospel with an Utopian fantasy is not only foolish, but it tramples the cross. We ought to run to the God of redemption rather than to man or man-made policies. Organizations like the NCC too often strip the cross of its offense in an effort to appear pious and loving. By doing so, the NCC and organizations like it will only confuse and obstruct the gospel of Jesus Christ. They should be applauded in their attempt to sow unity among the various denominations, but should also be vehemently condemned for promoting a false and shallow sense of salvation. The blood of damned souls falls on the hands of those who corrupt the gospel and replace it with a deceiving message that will never bring about the change needed.

Credo: I believe. But I do not in this so-called gospel that neither saves nor fulfills the commandments of Christ.

3

Twice the Son of Hell

An Atheist Visits Lakewood

A FEW years ago, a Jewish atheist visited Joel Osteen's Lakewood Church to see what all the hype surrounding the nation's best-known pastor and church was all about. Though skeptical at first, he quickly became a fan of the smiling preacher and the megachurch he pastors. Evan Mintz, the Jewish atheist, chronicled his experience at Lakewood from his perspective as a Jewish atheist.

Mintz first noticed the omnipresence of Osteen's best-selling books at Lakewood noting that they were "freaking everywhere." He then adds, ". . . but perfectly enough there were no Bibles. Bibles are so passé. The Bible is angry, judgmental and condemns everything fun in life – but not Osteen. Even after the ushers led me to my seat, I could not find any Bibles for those biblically impaired like myself. Apparently, Lakewood is BYOB—Bring Your Own Bible."[1]

The lack of the centrality of Scripture and Biblical exposition creates a church of ignorant, so-called Christians. Osteen's lack of Biblical discernment is apparent not only in his preaching, but also in his congregation. Every congregation reflects its preacher. Those who care more about modern psychology and Dr. Phil-ism will have a church more concerned with "how I feel?" than

---

1. Mintz, "Lakewood: All the Fire Without the Brimstone," lines 24–29.

submission to the Word of God. One is man-centric, the other is God-centric.

It is obvious in the writings and sermons of Osteen that the centrality of the Biblical text is absent and has taken a back-seat to a more feel-good gospel.[2] This does not mean Osteen rejects the Bible's inspiration or even its clarity, but in his practice, preaching, interviews, and writings, Scripture is downgraded in order to make room for a more Christianized, therapeutic feel-good message of self-esteem and self-fulfillment. Osteen has no time for difficult passages of Scripture that demand hours of study and the painstaking exegesis presented to the congregation. Why preach on the slaughter of the prophets of Baal when you could preach on the love of God and the power of self-esteem?

Osteen's ministry leaves one feeling better about himself but fails to further the gospel, preach Christ, call sinners to repent, or to disciple believers into a deeper relationship with their Savior. In other words, Osteen has become a mouth-piece for self-esteem cults, therapeutic societies, and prosperity preachers, but he has done nothing that gives God glory through the proclamation of the cross.

When one deprives the church of Scripture, it ceases to be a church. An emotional and spiritual experience it might be, but not a church. It would be hard to imagine the apostle Paul and the leaders of the Early Church being pleased with the lack of Bible exposition from the preacher and his congregation. In the last letters of his life, Paul repeatedly reminded Timothy to shape his ministry after the Word of God, defend the gospel against false doctrine, and to proclaim and teach a Biblical theology (1 Timothy 4:1–6, 16; 2 Timothy 2:15; 3:14–17; 4:1–5).

Scripture was clearly the guiding light and the force behind the ministry of the Early Church. Among his final exhortations,

---

2. Osteen himself said on Larry King Live, ". . . what I do is just try to teach practical principles. I may not bring the scripture in until the end of my sermon and I might feel bad about that." Transcript available at "Encore Presentation: Interview With Joel Osteen," lines 149–50.

Paul commanded Timothy to "preach the Word" at all times because "the time will come when men will not put up with sound doctrine" in order "to suit their own desires, they will gather around them a great number of teachers to say what their itching ears want to hear." It is as if Paul is speaking directly to our tell-me-something-I-want-to-hear society. Our ears are itching and we are not being disappointed when we turn on the TV and hear the gospel of me preached, bringing a smile to all of our faces.

After commenting on the worship (which he considered to be more of an entertaining stage show) Mintz goes on to detail a mini-sermon given by one of the female ministers:

"As the singing ended, a woman . . . started a sermon. Usually, sermons are bad because they make you feel ashamed both for sinning and for being ignorant of the Bible. But not at Lakewood. The woman just talked about how parents should raise their kids well. And apparently she knew even less about the Bible than I, considering her trouble recounting the story of Mary and Joseph."[3]

It is a sad testimony when those who rarely attend church pick up on the lack of preaching against sin. Lakewood has been given the unique opportunity to reach thousands of people every Sunday and millions of others through television and the Internet. Unfortunately, they squander this opportunity by being nice. Instead of exhorting parents to illustrate the gospel in their parenting, they simply encouraged parents to "raise their kids well" (whatever that means).

The Biblical ignorance of the church is especially appalling. If what Mintz says is true, it is scary that any minister at a church would have "trouble recounting the story of Mary and Joseph," who gave birth and raised our Lord and Savior Jesus Christ! If the leaders are Biblical amateurs, then certainly the far majority of the congregation would be spiritual infants unable to articulate the gospel or live by it.

---

3. Mintz, "Lakewood: All the Fire Without the Brimstone," lines 48–55.

Mintz then moves on to describe Pastor Osteen's sermon: "Then came the big show: Joel Osteen. With the audience cheering as he ran on stage, I could have sworn he bore a distinct resemblance to former Rockets forward Matt Maloney. As I saw it, his sermon consisted of three sections: Give money to Lakewood Church, if you're good you will get money and Joel is awesome. No surrender, no sacrifice, no sin."[4]

The impression of Osteen's sermon and his understanding of Christianity is very apparent to even the unchurched: prosperity and favor from God if you do the right things. Though Osteen may deny it, he is the poster-child of the prosperity gospel, and his hearers are picking up on it.[5] Mintz is evidence of it.

This presentation of the gospel and the message of Christianity could not be farther from the truth. Mintz is right to describe their gospel as "no surrender, no sacrifice, and no sin," but the true gospel says otherwise. How can one be saved unless he knows he is lost? How can one come to the cross if he does not know that Jesus died on his account? How can one seek Christ without surrendering his very will to Him? How can one die to himself and live for Christ without a crucified Christ? One cannot! Osteen may call it Christianity, but the feel-good, hug your inner child because God is love, spewing from his pulpit is anything but Christianity, and it certainly is not the gospel!

The gospel begins with our hopelessness with the cross standing as our only source of hope. The gospel is about us being broken because we are failures in God's eyes, deserving His judgment, death, and hell, and yet He redeemed us though we do not deserve it. That is the gospel. Osteen has left it far behind and has replaced

---

4. Ibid., lines 56–61.

5. On CNN Osteen said, "I don't like to be called a prosperity minister because I think in most people's minds that don't know me they think, 'Well, all he talks about is money . . . Which I don't, I talk about being blessed in so many different ways." Christine Romans, "Can Joel Osteen Help You Pay Your Bills?" lines 97–100.

it with a gospel that puts God under the obligation of men rather than men being under obligation to God.

Mintz adds:

> And it was amazing. All those Christian themes of giving into the will of God and begging forgiveness that make me so angry were replaced by prayers for money and success. Heck, even I prayed for my mutual fund to double, and I don't believe in God.
>
> Osteen continued to wax about how we should not condemn people for sin but be nice to them because that is the only way to change them. Also, he said, if you do this, God will reward you with a job promotion. Apparently, everything is related to money. From the begging for charity—not for the poor, but for Lakewood's first $10 million loan payment—to being a good person for the economic reward, Lakewood made it seem like God was just one big ATM.[6]

May God's judgment be upon any church and on any presenter of the gospel that leaves an atheist, or any other sinner, content in their sin. The Church has too often failed to plea for sinners to repent with the assurance of the forgiveness God graciously brings to their doors.

Mintz concludes his experience by saying, "After visiting Lakewood Church, I did not feel condemned for my sinful ways, damned for rejecting Jesus or even uncomfortable, considering the lack of crosses and Bibles. This atheist felt good. In the end, the only problem was that I forgot where I parked my car."[7]

It is a sad testimony of the American church when an atheist can leave one of our services with the response, "this atheist felt good."

Jesus told the religious leaders of his day: "Woe to you . . . hypocrites, because you travel around on sea and land to make one proselyte; and when he becomes one, you make him twice as much a son of hell as yourselves" (Matthew 23:15).

---

6. Mintz, "Lakewood: All the Fire Without the Brimstone," lines 62–73.
7. Ibid., 80–83.

LOGIZOMAI

No other words could better describe Osteen's ministry than those. Osteen will likely not be preaching on this passage anytime soon because it might offend the Jewish atheist still basking in the comfortableness of Lakewood.

4

Accommodationism Breeds Irrelevancy

Why Liberalism Fails and the Transcendent Gospel Triumphs

In search for cultural relevancy, many churches have fundamentally abandoned the gospel. In hopes of getting the culture to like them for the purpose of "reaching" them with the "gospel," many Christians have watered down the truth. Debates over contextualization, as a result, have taken preeminence over fidelity to sound doctrine. Issues like music, dress codes (or lack there-of), language in the pulpit, youth ministry budgets for ski trips and pizza parties, shorter sermons, and chairs instead of pews have taken a front seat in church debate. In an attempt to be faithful to evangelism, many have stripped the gospel of its offense and replaced it with a message of self-help and self-fulfillment.

As a result, liberal churches and denominations are dead.

Relevancy kills and thus oddly enough makes churches irrelevant.

In an attempt to accommodate, mainstream Christianity alienates. Throughout the history of Christianity, many have tried to model their understanding of the gospel and the local church after trends in the culture. Each and every attempt has failed. Ecumenical liberalism empties chairs and turns a thriving church into an anemic congregation.

LOGIZOMAI

The past decade has only added to the already ample evidence that liberalism kills. According to reports, denominations like Presbyterians, Lutherans, Episcopalians, Methodist, and other liberal-leaning denominations made up of 40% of American Protestantism in the 1960s. As of June 2006, however, the percentage has dropped to just 12% (17 million out of 135 million). Since 1965, Episcopalians have gone from 3.4 million adherents to just 2.3 million. Presbyterians during that same time period, dropped from 4.3 million to just 2.5 million members, and the numbers continue to fall.[1]

Liberal Christianity gets a lot of press but has very little real influence in the lives of everyday people. As one author put it, liberal Christians "have assumed a kind of reverse mission: instead of being the church's missionaries to the world, they have become the world's missionaries to the church."[2] In search of relevancy, mainstream congregations drop the biblical mandate to reach the lost with the exclusive gospel and have replaced it with a message of, "see, we're just like you." And so rather than being a beacon of hope, the Church is just another social club or humanitarian organization.

There are a number of reasons why such a message simply does not work. First, to base one's message on an ever-changing society inherently implies that in a matter of time the message will become irrelevant again. This is true no matter how often a church or denomination updates its message or chases the winds of the culture. To always change based on opinion polls and the

---

1. These numbers are based on an article from the Los Angeles Times. Charlotte Allen, "Liberal Christianity is Paying for its Sins," lines 35–41. The numbers were taken from the Hartford Institute for Religious Research. Dinesh D'Souza records similar numbers in D'Souza, *What's So Great About Christianity?*, 4. His numbers comes from the Institute on Religion and Democracy in 2005. He adds that the United Church of Christ went from 2.2 million members to just 1.3 million members, Ibid. Both sources site the growth of the Southern Baptist Convention during this time period from 8.7 million to now 16.4 million.

2. D'Souza, *What's So Great About Christianity?*, 3.

fickle wishes of society is to never be grounded in unchanging truth. Fickle theology never gives congregants the assurance and certainty needed, especially in times of trouble and uncertainty. Changing one's beliefs based on current trends is to possess no beliefs in the first place.

Secondly, by seeking to be relevant (by surrendering fidelity to Scripture and forever changing one's beliefs) one becomes irrelevant. Relevancy is not defined by how up to date one is or how popular their new tattoo is, but on how time-tested one's convictions are. Transcendence is more relevant than accommodation. A transcendent theology is a time-tested theology that understands the issues before they arise. A couple struggling in their marriage need time-tested, transcendent answers that work, not current marriage advice that may change the next day. A mother who loses her young son in a car accident needs a time-tested, transcendent message that brings comfort and hope, not words that sound like they came out of a parenting magazine. The drug addict, the legalistic father, and the abandoned orphan need a message that is grounded in something much deeper than cultural trends and the waves of society. What we all need is a message of reconciliation and hope, not a message calling for conformity to a fallen world.

Many have fooled themselves into thinking that hairstyles and music makes them relevant when in fact it only makes them trendy. When Christians, especially pastors and youth ministers, participate in this game, it shows that they spend more time watching MTV for fashion tips and Dr. Phil for counseling advice than they do studying God's Word and proclaiming the gospel. Christians do need to be engaged in the culture, but to let the culture define one's ministry and beliefs is to confuse relevancy with trendiness and trendiness is not the gospel.

Thirdly, when secularism is the dominate cultural worldview and the church accommodates it, birth rates become a serious issue. Secularism inherently undermines marriage and the family.

With secularism comes a decrease in marriage and desire for children. Thus, where there is secularism, birth rates will drop.

Lower birth rates affect denominations and churches because congregations grow as birth rates increase. When couples in a congregation (let alone an entire denomination) cease having children, the number of Christians will invariably drop. Religions, especially Christianity, have always grown based on reproduction rates and proselytizing. Christians are called to be ambassadors of the gospel to both the world and our children. By mimicking the world's deportation of children to other institutions rather than the home, liberal Christianity is signing its own death warrant.

Furthermore, an updated gospel foolishly believes that man can resolve its own problems apart from God. It is therefore a-theistic. The gospel begins with and ends with God. Justification by faith alone affirms God's exclusive work in salvation. To insert man and his opinions (driven by his depravity) is to take God out of the equation. Liberalism's gospel fails in both its transcendence and its anthropological assumptions. Scripture is clear that apart from an intervening God, man will forever rebel and sink deeper into the lust of his own depravity. By allowing the culture to shape one's faith and calling it Christianity, one contradicts the gospel. The gospel calls on men everywhere to repent and to be saved out of the generation, not into it.

Finally, a culturally-driven message is an attack on the doctrine of God. If the message changes, then the One who first gave the message changes with it. An ever changing message implies that God keeps changing His mind. To update the gospel is about more than styles of music or holes and stains in the youth pastor's jeans. It is primarily about God. If God changes with the culture, then He is no longer God. A right understanding of God implies transcendence. God is not limited to the wiles and fickleness of man. Rather, man is under the sovereignty and providential authority of God. Liberal Christianity, by changing and undermining the gospel, is guilty of dethroning God and replacing Him with the culture of the time.

Rather than cave to the wishes of culture, the Church must stand apart from it (Acts 2:40). What primarily separates liberal Christianity and orthodox Christianity is not doctrine, but transcendence. The "Old Old Story," does not need an update because it is not limited to time, geography, or opinion polls. Orthodoxy was shaped, not by a culture, but by God Himself before the foundation of the world. The gospel, therefore, transcends all circumstances, languages, races, nationalities, and cultures. The promise of redemption to those enslaved to sin is not limited to the will of the people, but is of the will of God.

The gospel is transcendent first because it begins with God. If God is immutable (or unchanging), then so are His decrees. An immutable God reveals an immutable message and in Scripture that immutable message is repeatedly declared. Persons are reconciled with God, not by chasing fads, but by humbly repenting of their rebellion against Him. To attack the transcendence of the gospel is first of all a direct attack against God.

Secondly, the gospel is transcendent because the need for salvation is transcendent. Genesis 3 records the fall of man which affects everyone. By inheriting the same sinful nature, the solution to overcoming and being redeemed from sin is also the same. Through one man (Adam) sin entered the world. Likewise, through one man (Jesus Christ) sin can be defeated (Romans 5:12–21).

Christian liberals are all too often more willing to place the blame of man's plight on some outside source other than human depravity. They blame systemic sin, environmental catastrophe, political corruption, socio-economic upbringing, or poverty rather than identify sin as the source of man's problems. Scripture is clear that all have sinned, all are guilty, and all have inherited this sinful nature. Sin, therefore, is transcendent and is apparent in all nations, peoples, tribes, languages, families, and individuals.

Since sin is transcendent, then so must be salvation through Jesus Christ.

Furthermore, salvation always came through substitutionary atonement. Immediately following the fall in Genesis 3 and the punishments God placed on humanity, God revealed the gospel through the shedding of innocent blood. Adam and Eve tried to cover their shame by putting together fig leaves (Genesis 3:7). Fig leaves were a temporary solution to a permanent problem. God, however, covered their shame by giving them animal skin to wear (Genesis 3:21). Animal skin involves the death of an innocent animal. Therefore, the shame of Adam and Eve's sin was covered by the death (an atonement) of an innocent animal.

The theme of sacrifice and atonement runs through the Bible and climaxes at the cross. The Day of Atonement (Leviticus 16) was the day that the sins of Israel was forgiven based on the sacrifice of an innocent animal. That sacrifice, however, had to be repeated every year by the priests. It was all a foretaste of what Christ would accomplish on the cross. There, Christ served as the innocent sacrifice in place of guilty mankind.

The point is to show that atonement has always been the universal solution to the universal problem of sin. Immediately after sin entered the world, atonement for sin was made by God. That has never changed. If sin is transcendent, then so is substitutionary atonement. When sin entered the world, so did the gospel foundationally seen in substitutionary atonement.

If sin and atonement are transcendent, then the universal call for repentance is transcendent. Both John the Baptist (Matthew 3:2) and Jesus (Matthew 4:17) called on people to repent. Following the ministries of John the Baptist and Christ, the apostles picked up the mantle of repentance. They took the gospel to various cultures, languages, and socio-economic situations throughout the Roman Empire. At every stop and in every culture the apostles proclaimed the same message of repentance (see Acts 2:38; 3:19; 11:18; 19:4; and 20:21 for example). Though every new city was a challenge, the apostles never changed the message, because the message was in no need of change.

Perhaps no other issue is under greater assault today than the transcendence of the gospel. When one complains about the exclusive claims of Christ and fights for a more inclusive gospel, it is really the transcendence of the gospel that is at stake. The foul of exclusivity is rooted in postmodernity and our obsession with tolerance. Transcendence is under attack. When one doubts the necessity or the historicity of the resurrection based on the impossibility of miracles, it is really the transcendence of the gospel that is at stake. A fundamental rejection of miracles is rooted in a scientific worldview developed over the past few centuries. Transcendence is under attack. When one claims that homosexuals can be as faithful to the gospel as monogamous, heterosexual Christians, it is really the transcendence of the gospel that is at stake. The rejection of homosexuality as a sin is grounded in a postmodern, sexually confused society. Transcendence is under attack.

Transcendence, then, is true relevancy. A fickle gospel helps no one and is thus irrelevant. So long as churches are chasing fads and updating what they believe to fit with the ever-changing times, it will remain irrelevant and empty. Let the declining numbers of mainstream Christian denominations be a message to all who are tempted to "keep up" with the culture. The search for relevancy enhances irrelevancy. Remaining grounded in Scripture, faithful to the gospel, and unconcerned for the trends of the culture, however, will breed the sort of relevancy and power every church seeks. The power of the gospel is that it saves and turns wretched souls into holy saints. The gospel does not need an update.

5

Freud's Wish Fulfillment

Why Atheism Cannot Explain Atheism

THE PUBLICATION of Charles Darwin's *The Origin of Species* changed the West immensely. The implications of evolution go beyond science to affect politics, morality, religion, and culture. Many Darwinists have opened up new fields of study, and the naturalist worldview that drives them presents new challenges that Christians must face. One of those fields is psychology.

Sigmund Freud is rightfully considered the founder of the modern psychology movement. His insights and the fruit of his labor over the decades has helped us gain new understandings of the human mind, but the worldview that drives it presents a problem to Christians.

Evolution implies that religion, faith, and theology are evolutionary byproducts, and many evolutionists have gone out of their way to prove just that. Religion, they argue, is nothing more than an invented aspect of humanity; necessary at one time, but irrelevant today. Proving such a thesis, however, has proven to be quite difficult. Freud's attempt at solving this riddle is just as problematic and his proposal is increasingly being rejected.[1]

---

1. One scholar writes, "Many of Freud's supporters have found such historical overstatements and simplistic generalizations embarrassing and irritating, not least on account of their erosion of Freud's reputation as a serious scholar and scientist. Freud, it must be remembered, was not concerned to

Freud considered atheism to be natural, not theism. He therefore argued that religion was nothing more than wish fulfillment that was invented as a means to escape the hardships of this world.[2]

Religion, he argued, satisfies our desire to live in a better, more perfect world. Freud's argument is logical when explaining why people believe in a place without suffering or hardships; no more pain, no more suffering, no more crying, no more uncertainty, no more confusion, no more death. Everyone *wishes* for such a heavenly place. Religion, according to Freud, has become the *fulfillment* of that wish.

But, how does Freud explain concepts like hell, sin, damnation, judgment, and wrath? Most of the major religions include some form of retribution. In Christianity, hell is the place of eternal punishment for unrepentant sinners. In other religions, retribution is seen in things like purgatory, reincarnation, and karma.

If evolution is true, then how does one explain the existence of hell and retribution? Evolution thrives on survival of the fittest which means that nothing is off limits. The name of the game is surviving, and in order to survive, one must do whatever it takes. Concepts like sin and retribution run contrary to such a notion. Doctrines like hell limit the liberty and domination inherent in naturalism.

In addition, Freud's theory implies that humans have invented a doctrine of worse suffering for eternity than what they face on earth. In other words, things will only get worse. How can evolution or psychology explain such a doctrine? It cannot. Retribution is based on the concept of a universal morality that can be broken. The concept of morality, justice, and retribution are foreign ideas

---

develop a theory of the origins of religion on the basis of a rigorous analysis of history. He already knew how religion came into being; all he required was a convenient (if largely fictional) historical framework to illustrate the theory in action." McGrath, *The Twilight of Atheism*, 73.

2. The argument is made in Sigmund Freud's book, "The Future of An Illusion."

to an evolutionary worldview. That does not mean that many have not tried to provide naturalistic explanations for morality, but at the end of the day, naturalism cannot explain the evolutionary advantage of morality.

Morality and, thereby, retribution implies a Divine Lawgiver. Thus the concept of law and justice is evidence for God. Evolution and psychology cannot explain the origins of the inherent concept of justice within everyone. Only God can. God, then, has revealed Himself and His character to everyone and only revelation can explain why doctrines like hell transcends time and geography. Christianity believes revelation came from God through the Biblical writers who wrote through the inspiration of the Holy Spirit. God's revelation is bound in the Bible.

No one seeking escape would invent an idea like hell; it must be revealed through general and specific means. Freud's theory may explain why liberal Christians do all they can to deny hell, but it does not explain why orthodox Christianity, and most other religions, continue to affirm retribution and why Scripture is emphatic about it. Everyone wants a happy ending. Everyone *wishes* for a happy ending. But apart from the gospel, there is no happy ending, only death, hell, and torment.

Perhaps Freud is onto something here after all. Hell remains contradictory to his theory, but atheism fits well with it. Maybe it's not Christianity that is a wish fulfillment, but atheism. By denying the existence of God and transcendent morality we all can *wish* and it becomes a reality: liberation from the shackles of religion, indulgence without consequence, and the right to be our own god. If there is no God, then there is no transcendent morality and no fear of a coming retribution. Everything, then, becomes permissible. Who does not wish for such a freedom?

This is a significant point: if anything is a wish fulfillment, it is atheism. Freud lived in a world of wish fulfillment. He rejected God because believing in God challenges our deepest desires. The best way to indulge one's flesh is to deny the existence of the One who stands as a judge threatening our autonomy. It is clear that man will do whatever he can to normalize sin so that he can swim in it and the most convenient way of doing so is to deny the existence of a divine being. No God. No retribution.

Though Freud remains influential, he has failed to explain the psychology of the believer, and in so doing, he has turned the argument on its head, showing the futility of the materialistic worldview. Perhaps the real wish fulfillment is really atheism, not Christianity.

The doctrine of hell, as it turns out, is not the threat to Christianity as it is oftentimes portrayed in Western culture. In actuality, it is the hurdle that evolutionary atheist must somehow explain. Hell is the one thing everyone wishes to explain away but cannot. It is engraved on our souls. Atheism, however, has become the epitome of wish fulfillment. So rather than shying away from or being embarrassed by the difficult doctrines of hell, wrath, and Divine judgment, Christians ought to wholeheartedly embrace them. The only explanation, as Freud's folly has shown, for the difficult doctrine of hell is God Himself and His personal revelation. The explanation cannot come from the wish fulfillment of men.

6

Piñata Theology

Ignore the Issue and Swing at the Distraction— What Piper has Taught Us About the Church

In August 2009, a firestorm brewed in the theological blogosphere regarding comments made by author and pastor John Piper about a tornado that struck a church where the Evangelical Lutheran Church of America (ELCA) had just voted to allow the ordination of homosexuals in their denomination. The firestorm came not because of the ELCA's decision, but regarding John Piper's comments about the destructive tornado. Piper wrote, "The tornado in Minneapolis was a gentle but firm warning to the ELCA and all of us: Turn from the approval of sin. Turn from the promotion of behaviors that lead to destruction . . . Turn back from distorting the grace of God into sensuality. Rejoice in the pardon of the cross of Christ and its power to transform . . . sinners."[1]

The reactions to Piper's words have been striking. He has been compared to Pat Robertson who repeatedly warns of God's judgment on those who teach evolution in school,[2] and blamed the catastrophic earthquake in Haiti on their "pact with the devil."[3]

---

1. John Piper, "The Tornado, the Lutherans, and Homosexuality," lines 49–53.

2. Robertson said, "I'd like to say to the good citizens of Dover: If there is a disaster in your area, don't turn to God. You just rejected him from your city." "Robertson: God May Smite Down Town That Voted Out Anti-Evolution School Board," lines 7–9.

3. See Bailey, "Pat Robertson: Haiti 'Cursed' Since Pact with the Devil."

Piñata Theology

Piper's comments have been referred to as "inglorious vainglory" that should be "discredited right out." Furthermore, such comments turns the Bible into a "weapon of ideology" who offers theological "crap."[4] Others have referred to Piper's post as "twisted logic" somewhere "between laughable and odious" calling on conservative leaders (like Timothy Keller and J. I. Packer) and conservative organizations (like Christianity Today) to condemn Piper.[5] Others simply mock Piper as a crazy preacher that should not be taken seriously.[6]

Such reactions are coming from evangelicals engulfed in a postmodern worldview who champion themselves as civil, inclusive, and tolerant, and yet are reacting rather harshly, close-mindedly, and hatefully. After reading such rants, one is left wondering where the postmodern tolerance has gone. It appears that the door of openness and love swings only one way.

The controversy in the blogosphere led Piper to clarify his original statement:

> Three years ago God sent the tornado of cancer into my life. It split the steeple of my health and shredded the tents of my sexual life. I wrote an article to myself: Don't Waste Your Cancer. It could have been titled: Don't waste your tornado. God's message to me in my tornado was essentially the same as to the ELCA in theirs ... In other words, the cancer-tornado was a merciful rebuke to my worldliness and a timely thrust toward holiness ...
>
> My tornado was a call to repentance. Yours will be too.[7]

Though such words were meant to clarify Piper's controversial statement, one should not expect the rants against him to cease. Postmodern evangelicals have a vendetta against Piper for

---

4. Drew Tatusko, "The Tornado to Stop the "Gays," lines 13, 15, 19, 34.

5. Tony Jones, "Who Will Call Out John Piper?," lines 10, 21, 22.

6. See for example Adam Walker Cleveland, "John Piper Contributes to Culture of Fear," and Jenell Williams Paris, "The Toddler, the Discharge, and The Humidity."

7. John Piper, "Clarifying the Tornado," lines 1–4, 17–18, 22.

reasons that go beyond his apparent declaration that God judged the ELCA. Emergent and postmodern Christians are the polar opposite of Piper theologically and stand contrary to everything he affirms and promotes. It seems that Piper's detractors saw an easy opportunity to attack and seized upon it.

At the end of the day, Dean Denny Burk of Boyce College raised the most important issue. Reflecting upon the controversy, Burk wrote:

> What are we to make of all this? What concerns me most about Piper's "evangelical" critics is that the direction of their outrage indicates that something is askew in their priorities. There appears to be little concern about the fact that an entire denomination has just taken a public stand against the Bible and 2,000 years of unanimous Christian teaching. There is scarcely a cross word about the fact that the ELCA Lutherans are walking away from the gospel of Jesus Christ. Instead, the critics are offended by Piper. Moreover, the offended have responded with what amounts to a lot of ugly mud-slinging—the very kind of stumbling-block to unbelievers that Emergents say they wish to avoid.[8]

Burk is right. The real outrage is not Piper's reflection on the events surrounding the ELCA, but the decision made by the ELCA itself. Rather than deal with the issue and what it says about their understanding of the gospel, many have turned Piper into a theological piñata. It is these sort of distractions that Emergents and Jesus-loving liberals claim to have moved beyond, and yet the minute they get the chance, they begin swinging at their next target.

The real issue here is not Piper's comments or the rants of his antagonists, but how modern Evangelicalism has completely missed the point. The gospel was attacked, not by Piper's article, but by the decision of the ELCA. At least Piper understands the necessity of repentance as foundational to the gospel for all of sinners, not just homosexuals. Rather than speak of repentance of

8. Denny Burk, "A Second Tornado in Minneapolis," lines 40–49.

sin and condemning the actions taken by the ELCA, however, the theological left has chosen to keep swinging at whoever they deem worthy or their bats.

The complete lackadaisical attitude towards the gospel should appall us. While the gospel is under assault many could not care less. But what else should one expect? By categorically denying the gospel itself, as many postmodern Christians have, no wonder the only thing newsworthy here is what that modernistic, right-wing, Calvinistic baboon (as they consider him) said about the tornado!

Christians must not get so easily distracted. Piper could have been more careful with his words, but what the Church is missing here is the effect decisions like the one made by the ELCA has on the gospel. It is ludicrous to expect men to repent when there is nothing from which to repent from. By not only tolerating, but promoting and celebrating open sin and rebellion, the ELCA has publically announced and affirmed that sin means nothing to them. To promote such open sin condones damnation as more preferable than offending sinners who will be separated from the God the ELCA claims to represent. So rather than be the watchman on the wall (Ezekiel 3), the ELCA and many in the postmodern and Emergent "conversation" have chosen to ignore the gospel and start swinging their plastic bats.

7

"Friendship with the World Is Enmity with God"

Rick Warren Tries to Have it Both Ways

WHICH MATTERS most to you: friendship with the culture or complete obedience to God? A Christian will not be able to please both crowds. Either the believer will be lauded by the culture as enlightened and wise or will disgust the culture and be labeled a closed-minded bigot and fool. Many well intentioned Christians, however, have tried to please and befriend both the culture and God.

Months after the 2008 elections, well-known pastor and best-selling author of *The Purpose-Driven Life*, Pastor Rick Warren seemingly tried to have both the applause of the culture and the approval of God and looked like a fool in the process. Pastor Warren had repeatedly been criticized for his stance against homosexual marriage and his support of Proposition 8 in California which, when adopted by the voters, defined marriage as being only between one man and one woman. Many attributed the success of the vote to people like Warren. Prior to the vote, Warren released statements that were clearly in favor of the proposition saying, "now let me say this really clearly: we support Proposition 8." In the same statement, Warren noted that "This is not even just a Christian issue – it's a humanitarian and human issue that God created marriage for the purpose of family, love, and procreation." He went on to "urge" Christians "to support Proposition 8, and pass that word on," concluding that "everybody knows what I believe about it."[1]

In this and similar released statements Warren made it unquestionably clear that he supported the passing of Proposition 8 into law. However, months after the vote and the fallout from homosexuals and homosexual activists, Warren apparently changed his mind. Warren came under attack as a closed-minded bigot who is prejudice against homosexuals. Warren came to support Proposition 8 based on his Christian worldview and interpretation of the Biblical text. Scripture clearly defines homosexuality as a sin and marriage to be only between one man and one woman and any worldview rooted in Scripture must affirm the sinfulness of homosexuality regardless of what the culture might believe. If one claims to be obedient to God regardless of the cost, then there is no wiggle room on this issue. A Biblical Christian must consider homosexuality and any other sexual perversion to be a sin because that is what the text clearly sets forth.

To change that stance results in a redefinition of the gospel. If sin is redefined, then the gospel becomes deluded. This issue is not just about homosexuality and marriage, but about sin and man's obsession with organizing, normalizing, legalizing, and celebrating his sin. Any worldview that stands in the way of man enjoying sin's indulgence will always be met with vitriol and opposition. The fact that homosexual activists reacted so strongly against this vote should not be so surprising.

The gospel is an offense. It is a smack in the face that attacks us at our core. We are wrong. We have rebelled. We stand condemned. No one wants to hear such a message. As a result, most will refuse to hear it. They will go further and condemn the gospel for being so condemning. Warren should have expected this onslaught from homosexual activists as every Christian should.

1. Brown, "Rick Warren Disavows Support for Proposition 8," lines 27, 40–41, 42–44. See also Gilgoff, "Rick Warren: Stopping Gay Marriage 'Very Low' on Priority List," and Bob Allen, "Rick Warren Says He Did Not Campaign For Proposition 8."

But Warren has changed his mind. Regardless of the evidence, Warren recently argued on Larry King Live that he "never once even gave an endorsement" of Proposition 8 and has "never been and never will be" an anti-gay activist. He went on to say that he never attended a meeting or "issued a statement" regarding Proposition 8. However, he did admit to King that he personally believed that marriage should be defined as "between a man and a woman."[2]

Warren seems to be speaking out of both sides of his mouth. On one side, Warren is clearly against any legislation that would redefine marriage as being between homosexuals. However, on the other side, he seems to be against such a stance. So which is it?

The truth is, it doesn't matter. Warren has clearly been affected by all of the name calling and verbal attacks upon him, his church, and his faith. Therefore, he is trying to show that he is not an enemy of the culture, but an ally and friend. The argument goes that to be viewed negatively by the culture makes it impossible to share the gospel with the culture. But one is hard pressed to find such a model in the New Testament. Throughout Acts and the Epistles, Christians are repeatedly persecuted, both verbally and physically, imprisoned, and killed over their message of repentance. Warren, however, finds such a model to be outdated. What we need now is accommodation and friendship with the world, not boldness and enmity.

Such a model does not work. The Early Church proved that more opposition leads to more converts. In the end, increased persecution, imprisonment, and martyrdoms were blessings rather than curses. By remaining faithful to the gospel, the Church increased. As for the times when Christians tried to be friends with the unregenerate, Scripture condemned them. The pattern is clear: opposition will only increase where the gospel is faithfully preached and obeyed. By apologizing for Biblical truth, as Warren

---

2. Brown, "Rick Warren Disavows Support for Proposition 8," lines 3, 7–15.

has done on national television, Warren has not saved his reputation, but has rather undermined the gospel.

As Christians, we must face the reality that the world hates us. The gospel is offensive. It stands in the way of personal indulgence. Anytime we preach or live out a gospel that is contrary to its offensiveness is the minute it becomes diluted and no longer redemptive. We must be willing to take the hits. We should all be ashamed if we cannot take a few verbal attacks when our forefathers in the faith were burned at the stake and turned into human torches by the culture they offended. Surely we can handle being called a few names.

So, will Christians remain faithful and obedient to the God that saved them regardless of the cost or will we continue to accommodate the culture and pretend to be something we are not? We cannot have it both ways because "friendship with the world is hostility toward God" (James 4:4).

8

Have We Forgotten the Gospel?

Glenn Beck, Social Justice, and the Gospel of Jesus Christ

GLENN BECK hates Jesus and poor people. Anyone following the reaction to radio and Fox News star Glenn Beck's call for people to leave churches that focus on "social justice" would be convinced that Beck is against the poor, Jesus, Christianity, the gospel, and America itself. In a world of sound bites and reactionary stars, Glenn Beck has come under intense scrutiny from many Evangelicals regarding his wholesale rejection of all things "social justice." On his radio show, Beck said:

> I beg you, look for the words "social justice" or "economic justice" on your church Web site. If you find it, run as fast as you can. Social justice and economic justice, they are code words. Now, am I advising people to leave their church? Yes! If I'm going to Jeremiah Wright's church? Yes! Leave your church. Social justice and economic justice. They are code words. If you have a priest that is pushing social justice, go find another parish. Go alert your bishop and tell them, "Excuse me are you down with this whole social justice thing?" I don't care what the church is. If it's my church, I'm alerting the church authorities: "Excuse me, what's this social justice thing?" And if they say, "Yeah, we're all in that social justice thing," I'm in the wrong place.[1]

---

1. Transcript taken from Grant, *Glenn Beck: 'Leave Your Church,'* lines 5–22.

Have We Forgotten the Gospel?

The response was immediate. Primarily led by Sojourners founder and the Emergent political guru, Jim Wallis, many have challenged Beck's reading of the Bible and the ministry of Jesus. They argue that the gospel is primarily about social justice and to undermine the call to social justice is to undermine the gospel itself. While Beck is calling for Christians to abandon social justice churches, Wallis is calling for Christians to abandon Beck.[2]

As Christians, a response is needed in order to sift through the fog. What is at stake here is not politics, economic theories, taxes, the size of government, poverty, or humanitarian aide. What is at stake here is the gospel. Though tempting to over-analyze and critique the various comments and responses of those involved in the controversy, Christians must not be so easily distracted. As believers in Jesus Christ, we must always be concerned with the gospel and nothing else.

Reading through all of the blogs and news bites, it is becoming clear that we are distracted by the politics. Unfortunately, many are confusing the gospel with a political platform? Beck is calling for his listeners to abandon the left-leaning politics of "social justice" churches. To him, "social justice" is a code word for socialism, Marxism, Statism, Communism, liberalism, and progressivism. The context of Beck's words cannot be missed here. Beck is primarily concerned with politics and clearly makes the connection between the words "social justice" as purely political. Beck makes a living fighting socialism, communism, Marxism, Statism, liberalism, and progressivism. He is no theologian and knows little about theology.

---

2. Wallis wrote, "Beck says Christians should leave their social justice churches, so I say Christians should leave Glenn Beck. I don't know if Beck is just strange, just trying to be controversial, or just trying to make money. But in any case, what he has said attacks the very heart of our Christian faith, and Christians should no longer watch his show . . . Beck denies the central teachings of Jesus and the Bible. So Christians should stop watching the Glenn Beck show and pray for him." Jim Wallis, *Tell Glenn Beck: I'm a Social Justice Christian*, lines 19.

The primary person mentioned in the above quote is important. Jeremiah Wright is a leading voice in Black Liberation Theology, which traditionally leans left and towards socialism. Furthermore, Wright's connection with President Barack Obama (whom Beck is not a fan of) is also important. Beck is telling his listeners that if their church or congregation pushes a political agenda of social justice (code words for socialism), like Wright's, then they should leave that church and instead attend one free from such radical political agenda's.

As a Christian I whole heartily agree with Beck (in this context). No church should primarily be about politics. This does not mean that one's theology does not have political ramifications. Theology should shape our politics, but politics is not the primary purpose of theology. Those leading the fight against Beck are showing their true roots. Though they may deny it, mainline Evangelicals like Wallis are modern day proponents of the 19th Centuries social gospel heresy.

Led by men like Walter Rauschenbusch, Washington Gladden, and others, the social gospel turned the gospel into a social movement that denied substitutionary atonement. The gospel became a nothing more than humanitarian aide and the fight to bring heaven down to earth via politics and social justice. Its leaders leaned left politically and turned the gospel into something it is not. As the saying goes, the social gospel is all social and no gospel.

When I read Wallis and others rail against Beck, I hear Rauschenbusch and the social gospel movement. Wallis is a political junkie that seems to only care about politics and how to use government to end poverty, fight injustice, and stop global warming. One cannot miss the absence of the gospel in any of his writings. He spends more time attacking other political junkies, like Beck, than he does contending for the faith once for all delivered to the saints (Jude 3).

Wallis and company are arguing that Beck is asking his readers to reject any church or religious institution that serves the poor or helps the needy. Are they really that empty headed? Beck's politics and firm belief in Capitalism is not rooted in his hatred of the poor but in his concern for the poor. The whole purpose of any political and economic theory is to alleviate poverty and create a better society for everyone. Beck's conservative and libertarian views are no different. Both Wallis and Beck want the same thing, but both are foolish enough to believe that politics is the answer.

My main concern in all of this regards how we are missing the gospel. In the fog of the "he said, she said" fighting, what we are missing is the gospel. The gospel is about propitiation, not politics. Wallis is so bold as to say that undermining social justice is to undermine the gospel. Certainly Christians are called to serve the poor, help the needy, fight against injustice, call for peace among the nations and among each other, live in harmony, volunteer and give to charity, etc., but that is not the gospel. For all of Wallis' and Sojourners talk about social justice and poverty, the propitiatory work of Christ on the cross remains absent from their writings, blog posts, interviews, and books. The gospel leads to social action, but social action itself is not the gospel.

Jesus Christ never ran for office. The Apostle Paul never complained about Caesar's tax code. The Apostle Peter never voted. Politics is not the gospel. These godly men and other early Christians preached Christ and Him crucified. That is the gospel. If we understand the gospel, then we can rightly live by it. Wallis and company are angry at Beck's attack on their politics. And in response have attacked his politics. How is it that we can call ourselves Christians and forget to even mention the gospel?

What Beck said is irrelevant. What Wallis is promoting is irrelevant. Christians are so caught up in politics that they have missed the gospel completely. Taxation will not eliminate poverty. Arms reduction will not put a stop to war. Health Care reform will not solve all of our problems. Politics can only offer a false hope. Only the gospel can offer peace and assurance. By turning the Kingdom of God into a social movement, modern day social gospel proponents are foolish enough to believe that the ramifications of the Fall can be defeated through power, government, and redistribution of wealth. As a result, the gospel is undermined and ignored. The Early Church voluntarily gave, not because giving was the gospel, but because they first had received the unmerited gift of Christ.

As Christians, we have a responsibility to serve one another, help one another, encourage one another, and fight for one another. But such social projects are not the gospel. The gospel is Jesus Christ and Him crucified. It is tempting to point fingers and get distracted by the political issues of our day, but those issues will pass with the next election. What people need is not merely cold water to drink or affordable health care; what people need is the gospel of Jesus Christ.

Glenn Beck does not hate poor people and to be distracted by such a conversation misses the point. Will Christians move beyond Washington DC and instead focus on Calvary or will we continue to react to the next thing the political commentator says that we disagree with? Beck's libertarianism is not the gospel. Wallis' social gospel is not the gospel. Repentance is the gospel and from the looks of it, a lot of us need to repent.

So I encourage you, if anyone is involved in a church that does not preach the gospel, leave now and never go back.

PART TWO

Culture: Where Reasonable Faith Meets Unreasonable Society

9

The Utopian Myth

Pandora and Avatar Blues

JAMES CAMERON's epic thriller, *Avatar*, has broken box office records with worldwide sales reaching over $2.5 billion. Cameron's previous box office movie was *Titanic* which made over $1.8 billion worldwide and was at that time the highest grossing film in history. Twelve years after the *Titanic* phenomenon, Cameron has released another movie that has grossed more money and raised more questions. There is something in the movie, beyond its special effects and 3D quality, that is grabbing people's attention.

Though most left the film entertained, many others left depressed. The depression is not based on the films appeal, action, or storytelling, but in the Utopian world director James Cameron created made up of the nature-loving alien race. Audiences are leaving the movie longing for the world so brilliantly depicted on screen knowing that it may never be realized. For some, it is hard to leave the perfect world of Pandora and re-enter the imperfect world of Earth.

The depression is centered on the confusion over reality and fantasy. Those suffering from "Avatar Blues," as it is called, wish that the world depicted on film was actual reality.[1] Transitioning from the perfect world of Pandora to our world of greed, natural disasters, violence, and injustice has been difficult for many.

1. See for example, Joe Piazza, "Audiences Experience 'Avatar Blues.'"

Pandora is a world of pristine nature populated by a race of beings that are intelligent and live in peace with one another. Such a world would mean unified families, the absence of natural disasters, and no more poverty. Pandora is the world we all wish to live in.

Man has always craved such a world. Though Pandora is the creation of writers, movie directors and producers, the ideal-world they created is not. Utopia is the dream of everyone born in this world. We all know that things are not as they should be; crime, injustice, suffering, natural disaster, war, poverty, famine, death, destruction, hatred, violence, bigotry, lust, rape, inequality, divorce, cowardice, brokenness, betrayal, hardships, dirty politics, broken promises, loneliness, illiteracy, discontentment, depression, anxiety, and disease are all a part of our world. This world is a mess and we wish it were not.

Discontentment in such a broken world has led to countless attempts to bring about such a Utopia. Various kingdoms in the ancient world tried to conquer their way to Utopia. The belief in racial and national superiority (not to mention the lust for power and wealth) led many political and military leaders to conquer, pillage, and wipe out inferior nations believing that if they were in complete control, there would be peace, tranquility, and Utopia. Peace through dominance was their mantra, and it failed.

Then came philosophy and Western ideals. The rise of the Greeks and Romans with the belief that they were superior to those uneducated and uncivilized. But rather than solutions and Utopia, it brought about more death, destruction, and chaos.

Then came religion. Christendom ceased being about repentance once it became the official religion of the world. Religion breeds legalism and tyranny, but Christianity was not alone. The rise of Islam and other faiths thrived throughout the Middle Ages. Instead of Utopia, forced conversions and heresy trials brought about continued violence, death, disease, and the cry for a better world. Utopia remained far off.

The Utopian Myth

Then came the Enlightenment and secularism. Many saw the imperfection of religion and sought to remedy it by running from faith to philosophy, science, and secularism. Many believed that the new world of scientific investigation and breakthroughs along with medical advancement would rid the need for constant fighting over endless theological debates and bring about a Utopian world free of disease and war. Instead, we discovered that for every disease cured, a thousand more replace it. As science advanced, so did the necessity to push the limits and soon scientific advancement led to more deadly weapons and new ways to kill. Furthermore, science, and the Darwinian worldview that replaced it, led to the practice of eugenics, population control, and racial superiority which led to more death, more violence, more disease, and more war.

Secularism also gave rise to economic theories like Marxism that promised Utopia once everyone was equal and shared their wealth. Instead of Utopia, the 20th century proved that communism breeds tyranny, death, corrupt power, and economic disaster. The high ideals of the 20th Century led to an increase in disease and more casualties of war than all other centuries combined.

In less socialistic countries, secular society's failed experiment of religion was countered with a cry to break from tradition. The rise of the sexual revolution, radical feminism, and racial dominance became the new voices of Utopia. By breaking from traditional and old beliefs, it was believed that man could be liberated and free leading the way to peace, love, freedom, and Utopia. The hippie's wanted Utopia and sought it in experimental drugs, alcohol, promiscuous sex, and peace rallies. Instead of Utopia, it brought about broken homes, an emboldened, less free government, sexually transmitted diseases, unwanted pregnancies, and the deaths of millions through abortions. Instead of Utopia we got moral relativistic chaos. And now many born in such a world roam the halls of Congress.

We have now moved on to postmodernism. Modernism failed in producing Utopia and has moved on to looking for more

Utopian promises elsewhere. They too have and will fail. The cry for tolerance, open-mindedness, relativity and the demonization of those who affirm doctrines without apology or fear promises to bring about peace and tranquility. A therapeutic world which labels criminals as victims and belief as bigotry has only encouraged added bigotry and crime rather than remedy it. Utopia continues to remain far off.

No wonder many who see a world so real on the screen become depressed when they watch the evening news. The cry for an Utopian world is part of our makeup. As Christians we understand better than anyone why this is: we were once there.

The Bible begins with God, who created the world in which we live, but not as we see it today. After creation, God declared the work of His hand as "very good" (Genesis 1:31). The day of rest was not the result of exhaustion, but of self-gratification for the glorious work of God's own hands. All that He had done and created was in fact "very good." A part of this creation was man who alone could enjoy the creation of God in a unique way. The first couple for a period of time enjoyed the Utopian, perfect world that God created: no crime, no natural disasters, no poverty, no inequality, no despair, no depression, no broken homes, no disease, and no death. Pandora was the handiwork of God millenniums before James Camera released Avatar.

And then it happened. Rather than celebrate and worship God as Creator, man sought to be the center of control. Once man was convinced that through disobedience he would become "like God" (Genesis 3:4), he never looked back. The motivation for the fall was set. Out of open disobedience and rebellion, man sought to be the center of the universe by dethroning their Maker resulting in the destruction of Utopia.

The story of the Fall explains why we long for such a world. Paradise was lost and we want it back. At the same time, it also tells us why we, on our own, will never recreate what we lost. We never created paradise in the first place. Scripture is clear that only God creates perfection. No matter how hard we try, we will never be able to duplicate the handiwork of God. The Garden of Paradise in both the beginning (Genesis 1–2) and ending (Revelation 21–22) of Scripture is the result of God's handiwork. Furthermore, so long as man remains self-centered, paradise will forever remain lost. The spark that led to this chaotic world was the belief that God can be ignored and we can be worshiped. By rebelling against God, our first parents decided to live for themselves and for their own pleasures. Pride and self-centeredness created and sustains our fallen, depraved, pathetic world.

The Old Testament is a rather sad, yet familiar story. Every page reveals how man continues to seek peace and Utopia and yet fail under their own ignorance and self-centeredness. Genesis reveals how man turns to himself, seeks answers in himself, and fails miserably. The giving of the Law created a people of legalists who believed they were perfect enough, but in reality remained just as depraved. Judges and Ruth reveal the utter chaos that liberty and anarchy create. Samuel through Esther show how power, corruption, and the lust for more inherent in politics destroys lives and any hope of Utopia. The poetic literature cries for peace and the end of injustice that always seems far off. And the prophets warn of coming doom as the result of man's actions.

It is a pathetic story that we all know too well. We, like those of old, have sought for Utopia in the same ways as they with the same results. Politics, unchecked liberty, legalism, tyranny, war, religion, secularism, and cries for peace have all failed. We continue to repeat the same mistakes of the past.

If the Old Testament was the story of the failure of man, the New Testament tells of the triumph of Christ. The Gospels narrate the triumph of the cross and how on account of the death of Christ, man finally has hope, if only they would give up their self-centeredness and repent. Acts shows the triumph of the cross-centered Church where love – real love – was central and unifying. The Epistles show us how to live such a cross-centered life. And

Revelation returns us to Paradise. Paradise was lost, but it will be regained not through human will or action, but through Divine intervention and fiat.

The central character of the Old Testament, one could argue, is not God, but man. Man is always seen as rebelling against God and trying to recreate Eden. The central character of the New Testament is not man, but Christ. The Old Testament is a book of man's failure in his attempt to recreate their Utopian paradise. The New Testament is the hope of Christ's triumph to bring about Paradise once again. Man failed, but Christ has triumphed.

Stories about "Avatar Blues," though at first surprising and almost laughable, should not be so shocking after all. The world created by the film makers is a world we have all craved and the resulting depression from our inability to recreate such a dream world remains. Yet only Christianity explains why we all feel this way and provides the answers on how a world like Pandora can be created.

Utopia will never be the product of man because of his self-centeredness and rebellion against God. Secularism is the same recipe we have tried before. No matter how lofty the ideals, it too will fail and man will realize that they stand farther away from paradise than ever before. A being bent on rebellion will never create peace. Paradise is solely within the creative hand of God. He must, and has, intervened. He must, and will, recreate Paradise if it is to ever become a reality. Our hope is in God and His gospel. Repentance shreds us of any self-reliance and self-centeredness. We cannot, but God does and will. Hope is not found in man, but in God alone. Will we continue the same failed cycle of turning to politics and politicians, unchecked liberty and promiscuity, legalism and tyranny, economics and science? Or will we turn to the place we refuse to go: our Creator who gave us Paradise in the first place? Only time will tell.

10

The Missing Story

Ida and the Search for Secular Validation

REMEMBER IDA? Ida was the name given to a fossil discovered in May 2009 that many eager scientists identified as the missing link. The media was quick to pick up and spread the story. With the discovery of Ida came a book and a host of documentaries suggesting that she was the missing link and thus Charles Darwin's theory of evolution had been validated.

We have been here before. Periodically a new discovery leads to claims that the missing link had been discovered and the media always reports it. Such "scientific breakthroughs" are always front page news. The cameras begin to roll, keyboards begin to type, and the world watches with glee as their ancestors are finally discovered.

But the story never ends there. Upon further investigation the discovery of the century turns into just another fossil. Ida is no different. Though those who discovered her gained their fifteen minutes of fame, the truth has been uncovered; Ida is not who the media said she was.

What is most shocking is the lack of media coverage the reversal of the facts receives every time. Just like the numerous cases before, the correction that Ida is not the missing link remains virtually unreported. To most who were aware of the Ida craze, she remains proof of the missing link because they remain ignorant of the truth due to the lack of coverage of the correction.

It is an appalling formula every time it is tried. Scientists continue to make wild claims about new discoveries and the media always reports it before a full investigation is made. They blindly buy into the craze only to be disappointed. Every time it happens those who gleefully welcomed the discovery are unavailable to report the truth.

But should we really be surprised by this? Every time the missing link is reportedly found the culture goes crazy, and when proven wrong, the news gets shoved under the rug. Should we not expect this?

What is at play here is not science, but a worldview. Secularism and the modern scientific community is built, almost exclusively, on Darwinian evolution. The problem with such a worldview, however, is that evolution has yet to be proven. The incomplete fossil record leads to uncontrollable excitement when fossils like Ida are discovered because all become convinced that their worldview has been validated. Its not about science, but about validation. But the discovery that fossils like Ida are not the missing link is a major cloud over one's worldview and thus gets swept aside.

What the media and the culture crave from these discoveries is not breakthroughs in science, but validation of their worldview. Darwin's theory of evolution is the foundation by which modern secularism stands. Relativism, sexual liberation, secular ethics, biotechnology, and abortion are all the result of a secular worldview grounded in Darwinian evolution.

Evolution shapes ones worldview and always has. Since Charles Darwin published his *Origin of Species* and later his *Descent of Man*, people have followed the clear implications. Thus when a new discovery is made "proving" Darwin correct, secularist and cultural elites alike feel validated, but when proven false it is simply ignored and once again they wait for yet another faked discovery.

Despite the repeated broken hearts of secularists, they continue to wait for their validation. The truth about Ida and all of the previous falsified finds should remind us of fallen man's desperation. To reject evolution by accepting its many holes would shatter the worldview of liberation for millions of people. So rather than acknowledge the obvious, many keep digging for fossils to validate their worldview. Ida is not an example of good science, but hope-filled secularism on the ropes.

The battle over evolution is a battle of worldviews and thus the war will continue to be waged. This is more about theology than science. To tear down the walls of evolution would lead to a reshaping of the Western world and a return to its theistic roots. Likewise, to abandon a Biblical understanding of creation is to redefine the gospel, robbing the cross of its glory and God of His throne. What is at stake here is more than just scientific investigation, but the future of the Western world. Which will triumph in the end: the gospel of Creation or the gospel of evolution? As yet another discovery gives way to disappointment we are again reminded of the Apostle Paul's words regarding a society that denies the Creator in favor of man-centered myths: "professing to be wise, they became fools" (Romans 1:22). And fools we have become; that is, until the next discovery and the search for validation will begin again.

11

The Personhood of Animals

The Argument Is Made . . . Again

A SECULAR society is a confused society. When evolution lays the foundation of society's worldview, virtually anything is permissible. Naturalistic morality is always relative determined by culture and evolution itself. What was considered wrong in previous generations is not necessarily wrong now. Without a moral foundation such as God in whom morality is defined and determined, a society is free to make up its own morality out of a straw hat.

This affects the core of American society and government. At its foundation, America has defended human freedom and liberty embedded in God-given rights. The Declaration of Independence clearly defines liberty as God-given, but when a culture becomes secular (based on its affirmation of an evolutionary worldview), how does one define and limit rights? Secularists do not necessarily question the existence of rights, but are oftentimes confused as to whom they apply.

This raises the question of rights for animals. For decades now, many activists, rooted in a naturalistic worldview, have fought for the rights of animals to be equal to that of Americans. To defend and protect animals from harm and torture is one thing, but to argue for the equality of animals with their human counterparts reveals secularism's confused worldview. Over the years, animal rights activists have fought and defended for some of the strang-

The Personhood of Animals

est causes. For instance, animals rights activists have requested that ice cream makers use human milk instead of cow milk,[1] they criticized President Barack Obama for swatting a fly during an interview and even gave him a bug catcher in order to prevent a similar incident from occurring,[2] and has called on the state of Pennsylvania to replace Punxsutawney Phil, the infamous groundhog that predicts the length of winter, with a robot for Groundhog Day celebrations.[3]

Perhaps nothing more illustrates the confusion of the secularist argument for animal's rights than "The Human Zoo" event at the London Zoo, which caged human volunteers with a sign that read, "Warning: Humans in their Natural Environment." The purpose of the display was to show the link between humans and animals. If humans are just highly evolved animals, and nothing else, then it only makes sense to display humans for bystanders to enjoy "in their natural environment." As Polly Wills, the spokeswoman for the zoo, explained, "Seeing people in a different environment, among other animals . . . teaches members of the public that the human is just another primate."[4]

It is tempting to laugh, but the participants and organizers were serious. Perhaps they left a few important details out. If humans are no different than animals, then why were only humans buying the tickets, organizing the event, and visiting the exhibit? None of the volunteers were captured by any primate or reptile and forced to live in the zoo, but volunteered their own time to make a point. Furthermore, how many of the animals at the zoo volunteered their time upon seeing an ad posted on the Internet?[4] Also, the participants wore swimsuits under their fig leaves even though their animal counterparts were not given such luxuries,

1. PETA, "The Breast is Best! PETA Asks Ben & Jerry's to Dump Dairy and Go With Human Milk Instead."
2. Associated Press, "PETA Wishes Obama Hadn't Swatted that Fly."
3. Barnett, "PETA Wants to Replace Famous Groundhog Punxsutawney Phil with an Animatronic Replica."
4. The ad can be viewed at "The Human Zoo."

being forced to walk in the nude. Finally, the humans went home when the zoo closed at night in contrast to the rest of the animals. The humans went home to warm beds, while the primates and safari animals stayed in their mock-natural environmental setting provided for them by humans.

Such an event, though laughable at best, should not be overlooked as insignificant. Only a secular society shaped by Darwinism would consider this a serious and enlightened event. The event, at the end of the day, was an attack on human dignity. One participant explained his reason for volunteering, "A lot of people think humans are above other animals . . . When they see humans as animals, here, it kind of reminds us that we're not that special."[5] Perhaps the danger of such a worldview could not be more explicit. When humans are viewed as merely human, and thus, "not that special," two misguided fallacies are promoted. First, humans are degraded by losing their dignity, making it logical to treat some humans as they would animals (primarily the impoverished, the handicapped, the old, and the unwanted). Secondly, animals are elevated to the status of humans, thus granted rights and legal protections uniquely enjoyed by humans.

Both of these extremes are visible in our culture today. When Atlanta Falcons star quarterback Michael Vick was arrested and publically shunned for his illegal dog fighting ring, a telling irony was missed. The West was outraged at the abuse and murder of dogs and yet not a tear was shed for the millions of unborn infants legally murdered in the United States alone. The abuse of the animals in the Vick case is certainly appalling, but the rationale for sucking the brains out of an unborn human or ingesting a pill that suffocates and starves a child is not questioned. The Vick case reveals the confusion of the secular worldview. By elevating the dignity and status of animals, while at the same time denigrating the dignity of humans, the culture became outraged over the treatment of dogs while remaining indifferent about how it treats its

---

5. Hechtkopf, "Humans on Display at London's Zoo," lines 29–31.

own citizens. A secular society without any moral foundation says much about the rights of animals, but says very little about the rights of so many humans.

So should animals have rights? According to some, animals like dolphins should have rights as "non-human persons." The leading thinker in this area is Dr. Peter Singer who teaches bioethics at Princeton University, whose firm belief in evolution has led to the conviction and promotion of animal rights, abortion, euthanasia, and even infanticide and bestiality.[6]

It works this way: evolution explains everything. Evolution implies some life is worth living and some is not. Those who are stronger thrive, while the weak dies out. How do you determine the difference between those worthy of life and those unworthy of it? Singer suggests that separating "human" from "personhood." Those declared persons should be given rights that should be protected. Thus, to kill a person is murder and criminal. To kill a non-person, however, is not. Not all humans are persons and not all persons are humans. Animals like dolphins, in such a worldview, are persons because they are "intelligent" and conscious. A fetus or an unwanted, handicapped child, however, are not "intelligent" or conscious and thus are not persons. They are humans but not persons because they are not intelligent and they are not conscious. To kill an infant with Down Syndrome, either through abortion or infanticide, is not murder because the child is not a person, just merely a human. However, to kill a dolphin intentionally or unintentionally is an act of murder because a person (a non-human person that is) has been killed.

---

6. Regarding bestiality Singer has argued that since we are all animals, "This does not make sex across the species barrier normal, or natural, whatever those much-misused words may mean, but it does imply that it ceases to be an offence to our status and dignity as human beings." Singer, "Heavy Petting," lines 88–90. Singer's basic argument is as animals we have no inherit dignity over any other animal which applies directly to our sexual ethic. As animals, it is not necessarily wrong to have sexual relations with another animal as long as neither party is harmed.

This clearly means that under such a worldview (a theology if you will), some animals have more dignity than the children of those who make such an argument. It is a frightening worldview to say the least, but one must admit that if evolution is true, then Singer and company are on to something. Evolution implies, and Singer correctly adopts, that human and animals are not different from one another. Thus, human dignity is an illusion; common ancestry clearly means that a monkey is a goat is a human is a pig. We are all animals.

In his book, *Practical Ethics,* Singer writes about the unethical protection of an infant born with Down Syndrome, even against the mother's wishes. He writes, "In this case a human being was kept alive, against the wishes of her mother, and at a cost of thousands of dollars, despite the fact that she would never be able to live an independent life, or to think and talk as normal humans do. Contrast this with the casual way in which we take the lives of stray dogs, experimental monkeys and beef cattle. What justifies the difference?"[7]

Here, Singer compares a handicap child to a stray dog, experimental monkeys, and cattle born with the purpose of being turned into a McDonald's burger. If we are mere animals, then what we do to some in the animal kingdom can and should be practiced against weak humans like Down Syndrome babies.

But not every human or animal should be relegated to becoming a Big Mac. Those given the status of personhood ought to be protected by the State (run by only human-persons of course). If some animals are also persons, then this means that humans have committed atrocities that have gone unpunished. Singer himself wonders, "Are we turning persons into bacon?"[8]

This is exactly the sort of theology that led Hitler on a rampage against Jews, the handicap, non-Germans, and many other unfit "humans" that he deemed unworthy of life. Grounded in an

7. Singer, *Practical Ethics*, 73.
8. Ibid., 98.

evolutionary worldview, Hitler rightly determined (according to his worldview) that the strong will survive while the weak will die out. The evolutionary Utopia could be realized once the weak are removed and only the strong reproduce without their genes being tainted with non-persons like the Jews and the unwanted.

Such a worldview leads to eugenics, abortion, racism, infanticide, euthanasia and other horrendous acts of murder. The foundation of evolution is that through death, a better species will emerge. Thus, persons like Hitler and Margaret Sanger (the founder of Planned Parenthood, who praised Hitler's eugenic measures) pushed eugenics in order to quicken the next stage of evolution. Only through pure genes untainted with handicaps, disease, poverty, race, or the unfit and unwanted can the process of evolution be hastened. Thus those unfit to live (non-persons) should be eliminated through means of abortion, infanticide, and euthanasia.

The birth of the contraceptive and abortion movement (led by Margaret Sanger) began with this eugenic mentality. Sanger was extremely racist and called for the extinction of blacks, the Chinese, and the poor whom she considered unfit for society. Sanger had ten other siblings and watched her mother die of tuberculosis. Rather than blame the disease for her mother's death, she "blamed the rigors of childbirth" and after the difficult birth of her own child, she became convinced "of the dangers of the birth process and the problems of poverty she associated with large families."[9] Soon afterward, she became a radical socialist that supported abortion, political assassinations, eugenics, population control, birth control, and contraceptives.

Sanger was devoted to Darwinism and his theory shaped her sexual ethic (and her call for its liberation from traditional values) and worldview. Sanger was only as radical as her worldview took her. She would go on to become the founder of Planned Parenthood which has performed millions of abortions since its

---

9. Schweikart and Allen, *A Patriot's History of the United States*, 531.

own birth. Though it is tempting to see Sanger as a rare radical, one must not forget the influence that Planned Parenthood has on the culture and our politicians. Many liberal politicians speak at Planned Parenthood events and forums hoping to gain their support, such as President Barack Obama who addressed the abortion institution during his run for the Presidency noting that "We know that a woman's right to make a decision about how many children she wants to have and when—without government interference—is one of the most fundamental freedoms we have in this country."[10] Sanger would agree. Likewise, in 2009, Secretary of State and former first lady Hillary Clinton was awarded the Margaret Sanger award from Planned Parenthood. In her acceptance speech, Clinton noted that the work of Sanger remains undone. So though Sanger, on the surface, appears to be too radical to be influential, she continues to shape the direction and policy of the United States.

Both Singer and Sanger are right. If evolution is true, then death means progression for society. The theory of evolution, the very foundation of secularism, opens the door to the rationalization of all kinds of confused ideologies and murderous efforts like abortion, racism, eugenics, animals rights, humans in zoos, population control, prejudice, infanticide, the loss of human dignity and sanctity, and euthanasia.

Contrast this with the Christian worldview. Evolution is a theology of death while Christianity is a theology of life. Only the gospel can explain why the face of a child with Trisomy 13 is more beautiful than the airbrushed photo of the model on the front of Cosmopolitan magazine.[11] Christianity sees beauty in all of life because all life originates with God. Dignity does not exist in the Naturalists vocabulary.

10. Toner, "Democrats Attack Bush on Women's Health Issues," lines 30–32.

11. See Mohler, "A Christian Vision of Beauty, Part 3," lines 2–4 and Mohler, The Disappearance of God, 67.

As for the rights of dolphins and other animals I remain perplexed as to why the obvious will not be admitted. If dolphins should be considered as persons and thus possessing inherent rights, then perhaps they should form a union, march on Washington, sing "We Shall Overcome," and lobby Congress for their rights. The very fact that only humans are having this conversation proves that God has made us unique. This does not mean that any animal should be mistreated or abused, for the same God also created them for His glory, but that humans—all humans— have dignity unique from that of the animal kingdom. And until animals hire a lawyer and lobby for their rights, let us treat them like animals. We should not lose sleep over the fear that we have turned the image of God into bacon.

12

Married with Children . . . Lots of Them!

SECULARISM LEADS to the demise of marriage and families. Secularism consistently redefines marriage and labels children as burdens. Thus, secular families increasingly do not marry and do not have children. A society cannot support itself with such trends. By undermining the family, a secular culture slowly dies out and gets replaced by another culture. Europe, for example, is quickly becoming Islamic because of this trend. Europeans refuse to get married and have children, while Muslim immigrants are getting married and are having five children each! It does not take a generation for such a paradigm shift to effect the culture.[1]

The Duggars, an American family featured on TLC, currently have nineteen children. Michelle Duggar, the mother, has been pregnant for over 14 years of her life! The Duggars are Baptist Christians who are part of the Quiverfull movement which does not believe or practice contraception or birth control. Though Christians can debate and disagree with each other regarding non-abortive contraceptives, believers should celebrate their willingness to welcome life into the world, train them up in the admonition of the Lord, and fulfill their ministry and calling as parents.

As should be expected, however, many in the culture do not celebrate the size and faith of this family. After the Duggars gave birth to their 16th child, Mark Morford ridiculed the family in lan-

---

1. The slow decay of secularism and the growth of Islam through immigration and reproduction rates is well documented. See for example Graham, "From Cross to Crescent: Islam Triples in a Decade," and Mohler, "Europeans Awakening to the Islamic Threat?"

Married with Children . . . Lots of Them!

guage full of more hate than one could imagine a tolerant liberal secularist could muster.

He refers to them as eighteen "spotless white hyperreligious interchangeable people with alarmingly bad hair" who are "worse than that huge 13-foot python which ate that six-foot alligator and then exploded." Furthermore, he suggests that the family photo on their website is so disturbing that "you will become rashy and depressed" and "will crave large quantities of alcohol."[2] The vitriol is astounding to say the least. The article is full of such strong language and utter hatred for this family. His hatred for the family is rooted in his anti-family, anti-religious secular worldview. On the surface, Morford is alarmed because he fears that each child will not receive the necessary attention they need. One must wonder, prior to modern psychology and pharmaceutical drugs like Ritalin, how parents in previous generations managed to raise such large families? Morford acts as if the Duggars are the first in history to experience the challenge of such a large family.

The fear that each child will not get their needed attention, however, is not the real reason for his diatribe. Morford, writing in San Francisco, is haunted by the thought that nineteen children (and now one grandchild) are being raised to be homophobic, intolerant Christian bigots. Morford shows the intolerance of secular bigotry. While disguising his concern as psychological, the root problem he has with this family has nothing to do with meeting each child's needs, but rather the fear that parents (religious Christian parents especially) have the right to practice their faith and raise their children not to be secularists like him.

He then wonders why "this sort of bizarre hyperbreeding only seem to afflict antiseptic megareligious families" like the Duggers. This leads him to ask, "where are the forces that shall help neutralize their effect on the culture? Where is the counterbalance, to

---

2. Morford, "God Does Not Want 16 Kids: Arkansas Mom Gives Birth to a Whole Freakin' Baseball Team. How Deeply Should You Cringe?", lines 24–25, 33–34.

offset the damage?"[3] Morford is at least honest enough to admit a fundamental problem with secularism. By undermining marriage and the family, secularism signs its own death warrant.

And people accuse Christians of closed-mindedness. Secularist like Morford see children as a burden (thus their unending love-affair with abortion and contraceptives) and families like the Duggars who celebrate children are only adding to the disease. Morford's real fear and the reason for this attack on the Duggars is his concerned that an entire "baseball team" is growing up to be the sort of people he hates the most.

But Morford has not completely lost his marbles. What lies even deeper under this hateful article is not just politics, psychology, or religion, but about the greater cultural war. Morford has to stop and ask himself what will happen if Christians continue to have growing families while secularist and liberals in America do not? Morford realizes that America will be subject to the same dilemma Europe currently finds themselves in, but instead of becoming Islamic, it will become Christian. And secularists loathe Christianity.

Evangelism is two-fold. First, there is personal evangelism which involves sharing the gospel with someone in hopes that they will convert. The other involves reproducing and raising a godly family. Morford realizes that if Christians continue to fill their quivers and secularists continue to abort theirs, a radical change in the culture will take place. All one has to do is look at Europe and see a once great secular society quickly become the next Islamic state.

Therefore, people like Morford see this family as not just an interesting story, but as a threat to liberal secularism. He condemns the Duggars because they are living out everything he

---

3. Ibid, lines 53–54, 58–59. Morford later adds, "Where is, in other words, the funky tattooed intellectual poetess who, along with her genius anarchist husband, is popping out 16 funky progressive intellectually curious fashion-forward pagan offspring to answer the Duggar's squad of uber-white future Wal-Mart shoppers? Where is the liberal, spiritualized, pro-sex flip side? Verily I say unto thee, it ain't lookin' good." Ibid 61–65.

stands against. So long as Christians like the Duggars reproduce at a higher rate than secularist, there is no hope of America ever becoming a purely secular society.

As Christians, it is critical that we recover and affirm a Biblical understanding of marriage and family. In America, people are getting married at a much older age,[4] falling for the European trend of not having children. Unless our culture, especially Christians, begin making marriage and family a priority, we will continue to contribute to our own demise. This does not mean that every Christian couple ought to have as many children as the Duggars, but rather that we must eventually, sooner rather than later, welcome children as the blessing from God they are.

A society that has lost a right view of children is a selfish society that has lost its moral compass. In our culture, children are considered a burden rather than a blessing. It is sad that such a story like the Duggars is so newsworthy. Decades ago, most couples had ten kids, but now the thought of having one child is dreadful and can be remedied through abortion on demand or the morning after pill.

Life should be celebrated rather than regretted. God's glory is seen in the smiling faces of little ones and in the teaching hands of their parents. In a society that honors the murder of children, it is refreshing to see a family that welcomes and celebrates them. The Psalmist was right when he declared that "children are a gift of the LORD, the fruit of the womb is a reward . . . How blessed is the man whose quiver is full of them" (Psalm 127:3–5a).

My wife and I have one son. I guess that means one down . . . eighteen more to go!

---

4. The average age for first marriage in American is 28 (men) and 26 (women). See Jayson, "Sooner vs. Later: Is there an Ideal Age for First Marriage."

13

Abortion

Is Common Ground Possible?

EVERY ELECTION cycle, the most divisive issue of our day is raised: abortion. Abortion remains a definitive issue of our time. For almost four decades, the two opposing sides have raged over the wrong of the other. In recent years, however, there has been a growing number of Americans who are seeking to reach "common ground" between pro-life and pro-abortion advocates. Many in this movement are led by those who label themselves as Evangelical and are followed by a number of other evangelicals. As a result, a biblical, Christian response needs to be given in light of this new and growing movement within the life debate.

But is common ground possible? If the two sides could come together and put aside their differences, it would stand as one of the most incredible compromises in world history. Politics would never be the same. The two sides directly oppose each other on abortion primarily because legal feticide is the offspring of two competing worldviews.

On the one hand are those that hold that all life is sacred because God creates life for His own glory and purposes. The fight over life, then, becomes an inherently religious one. The belief that God created human life in His image implies that all life has dignity and is worthy of living. Life is a gift from God and should not be taken away. To take a life is to murder one of God's image bearers (see Genesis 9:6). Therefore, the sanctity of life must be defended at all cost.

Furthermore, the human conscience is at stake here. A culture that rationalizes murder at conception can easily rationalize murder at every stage in life. If life is no longer sacred then culture defines who should live and die. Thus issues like euthanasia, infanticide, stem-cell research, cloning, and destroying frozen embryos are fought against with the same valor as abortion. Pro-life proponents understand that without the secular sacrament of abortion legalized, there would be no debate or push for similar life issues. Therefore, defending life at conception means more than just overturning a court decision; it defines the very direction of our country. God is the arbiter of life, not man or government whether inside or outside the womb.

On the other end, abortion proponents affirm a woman's autonomy over her own body. Government has no right telling a woman what she can and cannot do with her body. To have an abortion is a "choice" the woman makes and only she can make it. The government should not step in and determine what the woman can do with her body. There is, as the Supreme Court found, a "right to privacy."

There is also talk of "unwanted pregnancies." Children destined to be born into poor socio-economic homes or with handicaps (such as Down Syndrome) are unwanted, and thus most mothers are encouraged to abort their child. Children born in poverty are a burden on the tax payers and will likely live a life of poverty and crime. Thus, out of compassion for the child, such poverty stricken children should be aborted.[1]

---

1. At this point, many might disagree with this assessment as bias and untrue. However, one cannot study the history and arguments for abortion without realizing the eugenic nature behind much of the more radical pro-choice proponents. Prior to his inauguration to his first term, President-elect Bill Clinton received a letter from Ron Weddington, the lawyer that represented "Roe" in the infamous Roe vs. Wade Supreme Court case, regarding how he, as President, can cut down on poverty, crime, and health

LOGIZOMAI

Statistics show that children born with Down Syndrome have dropped dramatically (92%) in recent years, not due to advances made in medical science, but due to the high frequency of women aborting infants with the disorder.[2] Such a worldview suggests that children born with such conditions are unworthy of life based on their limited resources and quality of life. In the name of compassion, pro-abortionists defend the eugenic elimination of an entire generation of Down Syndrome and other handicap children.

These are two very different worldviews. One says that all life is worth living despite the causes of pregnancy or the quality of life and sees the dangers of the trending ideology that some life is determined worthy while others are not. The other hands autonomy to the woman allowing her to make the decision to terminate or give birth to human life based on any or no reason at all. Pro-lifers

---

costs in America. His solution was to eliminate such "unfortunate people." He went on to say, "And, having convinced the poor that they can't get out of poverty when they have all those extra mouths to feed, you will have to provide the means to prevent the extra mouths, because abstinence doesn't work . . . It's time to officially recognize that people are going to have sex and what we need to do as a nation is prevent as much disease and as many poor babies as possible . . . No, government is also going to have to provide vasectomies, tubal ligations and abortions . . . RU 486 and conventional abortions. Even if we make birth control as ubiquitous as sneakers and junk food, there will still be unplanned pregnancies. There have been about 30 million abortions in this country since Roe v. Wade. Think of all the poverty, crime and misery . . . and then add 30 million unwanted babies to the scenario." The image of the original document can be viewed at Weddington, "Weddington to Clinton," lines 19, 66–69, 70–73, 80–87. Likewise, in an interview with the New York Times current Supreme Court Justice, Ruth Bader Ginsburg said regarding Roe vs. Wade and abortion, "Frankly, I had thought that at the time Roe was decided, there was concern about population growth and particularly growth in populations that we don't want to have too many of. So that was going to be then set up for Medicaid funding for abortion." Bazelon, "The Place of Women on the Court," lines 3–7.

2. Dr. R. Albert Mohler has chronicled this repeatedly: Mohler, "Will Babies With Down Syndrome Just Disappear?," Robinson, "Mohler: 80–90% of Down Syndrome Babies Killed in Push for 'Human Perfection,'" Mohler, "'Pressure to Keep the Baby?'—The Descent Continues," Mohler, "A New Search and Destroy Mission."

are primarily concerned for the child, while pro-abortionists are primarily concerned with the mother.[3]

It is hard to imagine these two drastically different convictions ever being reconciled. Both convictions are rooted in opposite views of the world and theology. Therefore, it is unlikely that either side would be willing to compromise or abandon their convictions. Murder is murder. Choice is choice. There is no reconciling these two.

Or is there? There is a growing number of people, especially among more moderate Evangelicals, that believe that they have found the great compromise: Reduction.

Perhaps one of the major spearheads of this "compromise" is Emerging Church political guru Jim Wallis. Since watching the Presidential debate between Senators Barack Obama and John McCain in 2008, Wallis believes he is beginning to see glimmers of hope that this compromise might finally be reached and legislated. After quoting the two candidates from their third debate regarding their stances on abortion, Wallis noted that most Americans "believe the abortion rate in America is far too high but are hesitant to completely deny the difficult choice to have one." The solution, therefore, is abortion reduction which "could unite the pro-choice and pro-life polarities and bring us together to find some real solutions and finally see some results."[4]

Wallis and company see the partisan divides on the issue counter-intuitive to creating results. He argues that even after eight years of a pro-life President, who enjoyed six years of a pro-life majority in Congress, the result was not only failure to reduce the

---

3. This does not mean that pro-life proponents do not care about the mother. The opposite is true. Many pro-life organizations are dedicated to ministering and serving women. The point is that pro-life is built around protecting the innocent and the unborn. Likewise, this does not mean that pro-abortionists do not care about the child. Many would argue that it is out of passion and mercy that they seek to terminate the handicap, the poor, and the unwanted. The point is that pro-abortion is built around protecting the "rights" of the mother over the rights of the child.

4. Jim Wallis, "A New Conversation on Abortion," lines 52–53, 54–56.

number of abortions in America, but actually increased the numbers.[5] However, according to the Guttmacher Institute, the abortion rate reached its peak in 1981 at a rate of 29.3 abortions per thousand women. Since that year, the abortion rate has steadily declined. In 2001, President Bush's first year in office, there were 21.1 abortions per thousand women. By 2005 that rate had dropped to 19.4 abortions per thousand women.[6] Even with the correct numbers, perhaps the Reductionists have a point: despite over three and a half decades of pro-life work, Roe vs. Wade remains the law and the numbers of abortions each year are staggering.

The abortion reduction plan begins by addressing the problem of poverty. Wallis argues that three-fourths of abortions are the result of women unable to provide for a child. Therefore, Wallis seeks to make "both poverty reduction and abortion reduction . . . nonpartisan issues and bipartisan causes."[7] Certainly the plan makes some sense. Identifying contributing factors in order to prevent the underlining causes of abortion would certainly reduce the need for abortions in many cases. Certainly Wallis is not suggesting that all abortions are the result of poverty, but that if poverty could be reduced (if not eliminated) then so could abortion. The two are clearly linked.

But is abortion reduction the answer? The growing popularity of the movement suggests that many believe it is, including Christians. The hope is to find common ground and put the divisive issue of abortion behind us. But will this actually accomplish anything? How does one convince someone that reducing

---

5. Wallis, for example, argues: "Year after year, the number of abortions remains roughly the same, no matter which party is in power. The abortion rate actually declined a little during the Clinton administration, likely because of the improved status of low-income women, which is a consistent causal factor in diminishing the choice for abortion. But the abortion rate went up again in the Bush years, likely with the decreasing status of low-income women and families." Wallis, The Great Awakening, 193.

6. Guttmacher Institute, "Facts on Induced Abortion in the United States."

7. Ibid, lines 64–65.

murder is permissible when the very thought of murder, regardless of the rationale behind it, is repugnant? How does one convince someone that "limits" are the answer when one seeks liberation from limits? Yes, dealing with social and economic causes behind abortion are helpful and might reduce the number of abortions, but state-sponsored murder remains. Murder is murder, regardless of the numbers. Certainly reduction shows promise, but behind every number is an innocent life slaughtered in the name of compassion and choice.

Though Wallis' aim might be commendable it is naive. The idea that we can all get together, find common ground, and solve our problems reveals how blind he is on this issue. When speaking of life and death, compromise should never be a final option. Can we honestly say that we will be content with abortions cut in half?, two-thirds?, three-fifths?, nine-tenths? Even one life taken is reason enough to fight.

A broader look at the Emerging Church and moderate Evangelicals suggests that they have traded the priority of other social and political issues over abortion and other life issues. Though they claim to hold to pro-life views regarding abortion, they have placed issues like environmentalism, poverty, justice, and war over abortion. Such a trend shows that they oftentimes are seen as caring more for the planet than the life that populates it. This does not mean that these other issues are not important. They are all certainly issues that Christians should take seriously. However, many in the moderate Evangelical movement that have joined the call to just reduce abortions have done so as a sort of compromise in order to push their environmental and peace agenda.

Reductions are not enough. Resolving the social and economic causes behind most abortions are encouraging but it alone is not enough. Not all abortions are performed on poor teenage girls. If poverty vanished, raped ceased, and all handicaps were cured, abortion would still be common because the reasons for abortions runs deeper than economics and social status. We want sex but not the consequences. We live in a culture that is absolutely convinced that they can have one without the other. If one does become pregnant, there is always the option of abortion.

The abortion reduction platform only encourages the mantra of choice. "Do not feel bad," we console ourselves, "it's not your fault. You are poor and the child will be handicapped, he/she will keep you from living your dreams." By default, the reductionist movement inadvertently suggests that poverty is reason enough for abortion. They certainly would not affirm this statement, but that is the message that people are hearing. This is not pro-life.

We have been here before. Just like the world's first couple, we are trying to place the blame on something else (Genesis 3). We live in an illusion that sin and disobedience is never our fault. Though mistakes result in unwanted consequences, in this case pregnancy, that does not mean that God's glory is in anyway diminished. Only God can turn what at first appears to be a tragedy into beauty.

We must return, at this point, to the pro-life view. Because all life is sacred, we know that even challenging situations can still reveal God's glory. A mother uncertain of where the next meal is coming from can still find reason to smile and trust in a God who loves her and has forgiven her when her child's first words are "mamma!" And a culture that has for so long seen children as a burden can once again return to its proper understanding that all life is sacred.

God still judges and causes us to bear the burdens of our own consequences but He is also the God of love and mercy who always reminds us of His love even when we find ourselves broken, confused, hurting, and even contemplating or excusing murder. The gift of life is precious, and that can never be compromised. Abortion reduction proponents should be appreciated for their attempt towards peace and unity, but there are some things too important to compromise. Life is one of them.

14

The Anti-Choice Sinner and the Abortionist Saint

One a Martyr, the Other a Nuisance

THERE IS a double standard in our culture and it is no more apparent than in the tragic deaths of two men who had differing views on abortion. The first victim was George Tiller, a late-term abortionist doctor who was killed while at a church in Kansas. Tiller's death received wide press coverage throughout the nation and pro-life proponents universally condemned the killing as beneath their cause. All forms of murder is inconsistent with a pro-life worldview and thus the shooting was condemned.

The media spin was rather unfortunate. Tiller's death was used to demean pro-life proponents as his murderer was painted as the typical pro-lifer who was radical and bent towards violence. Pro-life advocates were described as religious zealots and violent extremists even though they universally condemned the murder. The media and the culture focused on the radical rather than the movement.

On the other hand, the murder of pro-life advocate and protestor Jim Pouillon has received less press. The motive for the murder was based on Pouillon's anti-abortion views and persistent protesting against abortion. What is most tragic about this case is that unlike the Tiller murder, Pouillon has received very little media coverage outside of pro-life websites. The silence is deafening.

The hypocrisy is apparent and striking. How is this not a story worth reporting equally as much as the Tiller tragedy? Here is an opportunity for Americans to be united under the right to free speech and protest apart from violence. Can we not differ and debate without the need of violence? The deaths of two polarizing figures in the national debate over abortion should have reminded us of the call to seek justice and debate apart from violence. Regardless of where one falls in the debate, violence should never be tolerated. Instead, we get loud laments for Tiller and silence for Pouillon. The murder of the late-term abortionist doctor was universally condemned by both pro-life and pro-abortion advocates and yet the murder of the abortion protestor by the hands of an offended pro-choice defender goes virtually unreported.

But upon further thought, should we really be surprised? A culture obsessed with death and the shedding of the blood of our little ones sees in Tiller a saint who died for the cause of sexual liberation and choice. Feminists unite. Tiller is a martyr that should be canonized by the culture. Pouillon, on the other hand, seems to be unworthy of our culture's attention. He is the enemy who has stood in the way of "progress" and women's rights. With the demonization of pro-lifers in our culture, no wonder no one noticed the appalling murder of "one of them."

While Tiller was canonized by the press and the broader culture, Pouillon has been characterized as a right-wing radical. For example, shortly after the Pouillon murder, one news organization described the victim as an "radical" and "committed,"[1] and as one who "had [an] extensive background of civil violations."[2]

---

1. Shaw, "Former Co-Worker Describes Dead Anti-Abortion Activist, Killed Friday Morning in Front of Owosso High School, as Radical and Committed," lines 11, 14.

2. Shaw, "Homicide Victim James Pouillon Had Extensive Background of Civil Violations, Many Related to Anti-Abortion Protest," title.

Should we really be surprised by all of this? With a culture whose hands are stained with blood, what is one more unwanted life; especially one who vehemently opposed and fought against the first and foremost sacrament of the Church of Western Secularism? Why care about the murder of an innocent man when we defend, promote, and celebrate the decapitation of an entire generation without a sigh?

15

Where Does the Madness End?

The Dire Destination of the Homosexual Agenda—Part 1

WHERE WILL the sexual liberation madness end? It is foolish to think that legalizing same-sex marriage would end the debate over the definition of marriage, the qualifications for civil unions, or the legality of limiting marriage to certain sexual preferences. Whenever a culture, especially a postmodern culture, begins to redefine something as central as marriage it struggles to come to a final definition. In other words, if we redefine marriage to allow homosexuals, why not other sexual lifestyles? Why should the debate over marriage stop at homosexuality? Cannot the same arguments be made for polygamy or any other sexual lifestyle? Why can we not lower the age of consent like other nations? What is to stop us from sinking lower and lower into the abominable filth of sexual confusion?

Or what about giving civil union rights to . . . friends? The argument is being made that the same civil rights that married couples enjoy should be given to close friends. Proponents suggest that it is unfair and prejudice that only romantic couples have the right to take advantage of the Family and Medical Leave Act which allows couples to share legal rights which involves mutual rights and privileges as well as various tax benefits.

Where Does the Madness End?

One might quickly notice the echoed arguments made by homosexual activist. Homosexuals argue that it is prejudice that they are prevented from sharing the same civil rights as heterosexuals. To be denied civil unions is a form of discrimination. Why can the same argument not be used for other sexual (or even nonsexual) lifestyles? Why can close friends not take off work to take care of their sick friend? Why can a couple involving a minor not be allowed to exercise the same civil rights of heterosexual couples so long as it is consensual and both parties are in "love?"

Dinesh D'Souza made this argument in his book, *Letters To A Young Conservative*. While a college student at Dartmouth, the university refused to stop funding a gay society despite complaints from conservative students. But rather than just complain to the university, *The Dartmouth Review*, a conservative student paper, decided to get even by forming the Dartmouth Bestiality Society. This society appointed a president, a vice president, a treasurer, and even a zookeeper. After developing a budget and writing up an application, the mock society went before the university and made their case. D'Souza describes their reaction:

> The administrators were appalled, of course. "There is no interest in, ahem, bestiality at Dartmouth," one said. To which the president of the Bestiality Society gamely replied, "That may be true, Dean Hanson, but it is because of centuries of discrimination! Those of us who are inclined toward animals have been systematically excluded and ostracized. Our organization will provide a supportive atmosphere in which people of our particular sexual orientation are treated with respect. At Dartmouth, if not in society, let us put an end to beastophobia."[1]

Obviously, the society did not get the funding they were seeking, but they did make their point beautifully. The society sought to illustrate the absurdity of the university's policies. They showed that the arguments used by the university to rationalize its funding of the gay society apply to any and all sexual lifestyles including bestiality. The society wanted the university to say no in order to

1. D'Souza, *Letters to a Young Conservative*, 28.

illustrate their double standard. So though the conservatives at Dartmouth heading the Bestiality group were comically serious, why did the administration not allow the funding of their group? Same arguments, proposals, purposes, and benefits. Are they not people with needs too?

When culture begins to redefine marriage, it becomes impossible to come to a final definition. In some states, homosexuals have been able to redefine marriage to fit their sexual lifestyle but why should the madness stop there? Should society not end the centuries of bigotry and include other sexual lifestyles as well? The same argument used for gays in America opens the door for other sexual lifestyles to gain the same recognition.

This slippery slope is applied in the defense of civil unions for friends. Those proposing these civil unions begin, as the homosexual movement does, with the trend in recent decades of the changing landscape of American marriage. In her article defending civil unions for friends, Rebecca Tuhus-Dubrow notes that "Over the past few decades, the laws governing marriage and family have shifted. In the 1960s and 1970s, a series of landmark reforms made marriage a radically different institution: women were granted equal rights within marriage, 'illegitimate' children were granted legal rights, and no-fault divorce made dissolving a marriage much easier. More recently, a number of states have created civil unions and domestic partnerships.[2]

By tracing the evolution of marriage in our culture, things like no-fault divorce have made "dissolving" marriage much easier while the creation of civil unions have allowed many to take advantage of the benefits of marriage without the commitment of marriage. As a result, marriage becomes a certificate from the government rather than a covenant made before God. The dissolving of marriage has led to a fundamental shift in the definition of marriage. But it does not stop there, notice where the argument leads in the next paragraph:

2. Tuhus-Dubrow, "I Now Pronounce You . . . Friend and Friend: Some Argue It's Time to Legally Recognize the Bond of Friendship," page 2, lines 24–29.

Where Does the Madness End?

> In the view of some analysts . . . the reforms haven't gone far enough – the law now needs to catch up to the society it helped to shape, in which many more people live outside marriage. The reforms . . . have even begun to recognize committed romantic relationships between members of the same sex. But for the most part, the law hasn't acknowledged the other types of important relationships that people can form.
>
> "If the law decides to support some relationships, why not others that similarly involve care and support?" asks Washington University's [Laura] Rosenbury. "What is it about marriage or marriage-like relationships—that is, relationships that are assumed to have sex in them?"[3]

If we follow the logic that begins by redefining marriage, one must admit that they have a point. Why can friends and other sexual lifestyles not enjoy the benefits of civil unions that heterosexuals (married or not) enjoy today? The point is, there is no end to this hill we are rolling down by redefining marriage in the name of equality and ending centuries of "prejudice." Therefore, the line must be drawn in the sand somewhere. If only we would have the stomach to do so even if we occasionally offend someone. Our fear of hurting someone's feelings is destroying our moral ability to take a stand.

The passing of civil unions among friends is the least of our worries. However, we must realize that once society begins down this slippery slope, there will be no end to the continual redefinition of marriage and the further push for sexual liberation. Homosexuality is not the end of the story. Christians deserve some of the blame for this slippery slope. Instead of preserving our own marriages, we have resembled our confused culture by the multiple divorces within our church walls. By not preserving marriage, we too have contributed to its decay. The good news is, the preservation of marriage is possible and it begins with Christians taking their marriages more seriously and with the preaching of the gospel. Repentance affects both the marriages on the rocks, and those still waiting for changes in the law. Where will the madness end? At this rate, it never will.

3. Ibid., lines 30–40.

16

Where Does the Madness End?

Where the Homosexual Agenda Leads—Part 2

IN THE previous chapter we discussed the endless game of redefining marriage. The real danger in the debate over the meaning and limits of marriage, however, has nothing to do with its definition, but how a secular society responds to opposition to their sexual liberation after it has been normalized and legalized. As history and current events and trends reveal, America is quickly on the verge of censoring, prosecuting, and persecuting proponents of traditional marriage.

Though it seems farfetched now, Christians must open their eyes and brace themselves for the storm quickly heading their way. A culture bent on inclusivity and "tolerance" will show its wrath on those who remain "locked" in the past and challenge its sexual deviancy. This means that the Body of Christ will become the enemy of the depraved culture once gay marriage is accepted. History has revealed that the legalization of homosexual marriage is the launching pad of Christian persecution in secular cultures. America will be no different.

Where Does the Madness End?

Those who stand in the way of pushing homosexuality and other sexual lifestyles forward will be met with legal resistance. Many books have already chronicled the many trials, imprisonments, and accusations of hate speech and other hate crimes against those who oppose alternative sexual lifestyles. In a similar vein an article titled, "The Coming Persecution: How Same-Sex 'Marriage' Will Harm Christians," author Charles Colson traces the persecution of several persons and groups who have been silenced due to their opposition to gay marriage. For example, a Methodist retreat center in New Jersey had their tax-exempt status annulled when they refused to allow two lesbian couples access to their pavilion for a civil union ceremony.[1]

Likewise, in Massachusetts, where gay marriage was legalized through judicial fiat, Catholic Charities were ordered to accept homosexual couples as candidates for adoption. Rather than comply with the order, Catholic Charities closed its adoption program.[2]

More frightening is that the homosexual agenda has reached the public schools and in virtually every outrageous case, the purpose of the indoctrination is to raise awareness, to teach diversity, and to encourage tolerance of persons with alternative lifestyles. Colson writes that "California public schools have been told they must be 'gay friendly.'"[3] One example of such a policy is the Alameda Unified School District which has forced its elementary students, even without their parents' permission, to attend classes that teach about homosexual, transgender, and bisexual families.[4]

1. For more on this story see, Capuzzo, "Group Loses Tax Break Over Gay Union Issue." The article notes that "In a letter dated Saturday that revoked the longstanding certification, [Lisa] Jackson, the environmental protection commissioner, wrote, 'It is clear that the pavilion is not open to all persons on an equal basis.'" Ibid., 24–26.

2. For more on this story see, Wen, "Catholic Charities Stuns State, Ends Adoptions."

3. Colson, "The Coming Persecution: How Same-Sex 'Marriage' Will Harm Christians," line 22.

4. For more on this story see, "Angry Parents Suing California Schools Over Mandatory Gay-Friendly Classes."

But it is not just California public schools that spread homosexual values apart from parent discretion. In 2002, Pioneer High School in Ann Arbor, Michigan celebrated diversity week which involved a panel discussion on topics like "Homosexuality and Religion."

> The school required students to submit the text of their speeches to the administration for approval. When student Betsy Hansen submitted her speech, school officials removed all remarks critical of homosexuality. Betsy was also forbidden to articulate her Roman Catholic view on homosexuality during the panel discussion—even though the panel was supposed to talk about homosexuality and religion. Officials informed her that her 'negative' message would conflict with and 'water down' the 'positive' religious message they were trying to convey—that religion and homosexual behavior are compatible and that homosexual behavior is neither sinful nor immoral.[5]

Even the Mennonites are not safe from legal persecution for not tolerating the homosexual agenda. In Quebec, the government informed a Mennonite school "that it must conform to providential law regarding curriculum . . . that teaches children that homosexuality is a valid lifestyle." Colson then wonders, "How long will it be before the U.S. government goes after private schools?"[6]

Even the Universities are under attack. Colson details how the associate vice president for human resources at the University of Toledo was fired for voicing her disapproval of homosexuality by writing an article in the Toledo Free Press in which she came out in support of traditional marriage.[7]

What we have here is a systematic outlawing of the First Amendment for those who stand in the way of the gay agenda. But

---

5. Limbaugh, *Persecution*, 101–2.

6. Colson, "The Coming Persecution: How Same-Sex 'Marriage' Will Harm Christians," lines 23–25.

7. For more on this story see, Burkhardt, "Crystal Dixon Sues UT for Rights Violation." See also Dixon, "Gay Rights and Wrongs: Another Perspective."

these examples are rather tame compared to others that could be chronicled. Not all forms of persecution against Christians for their opposition to homosexuality comes at the hands of government. For example, shortly after the passing of Proposition 8, a group of homosexuals in San Francisco verbally and physically assaulted a group of Christians while they were praying. Demonstrating rage after losing the Proposition 8 battle, the gay activists cornered the Christians and proceeded to shove, kick, assault, and even splash hot coffee on their faces. To make matters worse, during the assault, some in the mob tried to sodomize the Christians in the midst of the chaos. And there was no national outcry.[8]

Similarly, during a Michigan church service, a mob of thirty gay activists stormed the church with protesters inside and outside the church shouting things like, "Jesus was a homo." The mob then proceeded to pull the fire alarm causing the congregants to flee the church at which the mob hung up a banner in the pulpit that said, "ITS OKAY TO BE GAY! BASH BACK!" Furthermore, "the church was vandalized, obscenities were shouted and worshippers were confronted. According to Right Michigan the protestors in their demonstration also used condoms, glitter, confetti, and pink fabric . . . [Furthermore] approximately an hour after the demonstration two of the demonstrators were found by security in a public restroom in the church together. There were no arrests."[9]

Again, there was no national outcry.

Gay activists understand that in order for their agenda to succeed, there can be no opposition and in order to rid themselves of opposition, they must resort to name calling, silencing their critics especially through legislative means, and sometimes even violence (as illustrated above). First, the name calling. Opponents to homosexuality, transgenderism, and other sexual lifestyles are

---

8. Hoffman, "Christian Prayer Group Sexually and Physically Assaulted by Homosexual Mob."

9. Jalsevac, "Homosexualist Anarchists Storm Michigan Church During Sunday Service," 18–22.

accused of bigotry, intolerance, and close-mindedness. In a postmodern society such name tags could not be a worse indictment. And since opponents are considered bigots and homophobes, they are, therefore, inciting hate.

The problem with this argument is that it is self-refuting. To call someone a bigot is in itself bigoted and to say someone is intolerant is itself intolerant. Though this should be obvious, the culture conveniently determines the code of ethics in society. Therefore, to disagree with the culture and its predetermined ethics is to be divisive, angry, bigoted, and inciting hate. Name calling is a strategic way of winning the debate without actually having one. No one wants to be labeled intolerant or bigoted, and therefore many simply remain silent. Interestingly, what this does is intolerantly shut out opposition in order to give oneself the label of tolerance. By tolerance, the culture means for others to accept them without the intention of ever accepting those who disagree with them.

This is why the effort is made to convince Americans that homosexuality is not a choice, but a symbol of liberation from a past of bigotry and hate. It has taken on the mantra of a civil right where Harvey Milk has become the new Martin Luther King, Jr. In order to make the comparison with racial equality, millions of dollars has been spent searching for the "gay gene." If homosexuality is predetermined at birth by our genes, then homosexuality is not a choice but a right. Once the culture is convinced that homosexuality is something one is born with, and therefore an uncontrollable lifestyle, then such name calling points to criminal activity. Just as those against equal rights for blacks are referred to as racist and thus inciting hate, those who are against equal rights for homosexuals are labeled homophobes and are guilty of the same.[10]

Second, those who stand against the homosexual agenda will be penalized. As Colson and others point out, many are being

10. A good example of this is the Proposition 8 trial where the plaintiffs argued that homosexuality is not a choice, but is determined at birth. Therefore, the passing of Proposition 8, which defined marriage as being between one man and one woman, is illegal, infringing on the civil rights homosexuals.

persecuted and prosecuted for exercising their First Amendment right by speaking out against alternative sexual lifestyles. With the passing of hate speech and other hate crime laws our culture is increasingly becoming intolerant to other points of view. Hate crime legislation never insures liberty, it smothers it.

This, too, is hypocritical. Our culture repeatedly prides itself on being open and tolerant, but only applies such tolerance to those who agree with them. That is not tolerance, but censorship. Our culture will only tolerate their desired template and anyone who sails off course will be dealt with accordingly. The reason Christians are so hated is because they have failed to walk in line with the "tolerant" ethics of the culture. And in a culture where sex is the closest thing to a sacrament, to not tolerate unrestrained licentiousness is to incite hate.

By declaring a sexual lifestyle as immoral, Christians are accused of racial-like slurs where gays claim to feel like second-class citizens. What such an argument fails to realize is that to equate disapproval with second-class degradation is itself to denigrate those you disagree with as second-class citizens. By setting the rules, the homosexual movement has convinced millions of Americans that by limiting marriage to just one man and one woman makes homosexuals less of an American. However, taken to its logical end, to punish traditional marriage proponents for holding such a view makes heterosexuals less American. The pendulum swings both ways.

The hate crime laws slowly being passed in the secular West shows just how far a secular society is willing to go to silence opposition especially when sexual liberation is at stake. Secularism, as the 20th Century revealed, is stained with the blood of its opponents. This does not mean that America or the West is like the Soviets or the Nazi's, but that historically, secular societies censor, persecute, prosecute, and silence any opposition. It has a history of executing freedom in the name of tolerance and unity. Secularism is inherently intolerant.

We should expect the persecution of the church over the bedroom to increase in the coming years with no end in sight. Unless America wakes from her dream of equality for all people despite the abomination of its morals, the Church in America will never remain free. Censorship, prosecution, and violence is the offspring of secularism and we are quickly headed down that path.

But the Church need not be worried. Christianity thrives on persecution. At no point in her history has the Church ever suffered from persecution. Rather, God has always honored faithful obedience, even in the face of legal opposition and tyranny, by the repentance of believers. As one early Church Father said, "the blood of the martyrs is the seed of the Church." When the world sees authenticity in believers, and not the fake-Christianity so prevalent today, people come to Christ in droves. So though there is much reason to fear, there is more reason to rejoice. Our generation could be the generation with less freedom, but with more converts. So while the future looks bleak, we have much to look forward to. The Kingdom of God is at hand!

17

Punishing Prejudice by Being Prejudice

The Lesson and Legacy of Hate Crimes

O F THE many laws in our country, perhaps the most controversial and ambiguous are laws against hate. Exactly how one defines a hate crime is a matter of opinion. To prosecute a hate crime oftentimes threatens Constitutional protections such as free speech, freedom of religion, and the freedom of expression. It furthermore threatens the separation of State and Church by allowing the State to regulate sermons, speech, and public discourse. Therefore, to pass hate crime bills, the bill must be very specific (thus prejudice) or ambiguous (thus open for interpretation). Both can be dangerous.

In 2009, US Attorney General Eric Holder was asked a hypothetical question regarding a hate crimes bill, known as the Matthew Shepard and James Byrd, Jr. Hate Crimes Prevention Act which was signed into law by President Barack Obama on October 28, 2009, and how it would be prosecuted. If a homosexual was attacked because of a pastor's sermon would the pastor be guilty of a hate crime? Holder answered yes. But if a pastor was attacked by a homosexual would the proposed hate crime bill protect the pastor? Holder admitted that it would not. He explains the double standard on the grounds that the bill primarily protects "crimes that have a historic basis. Groups who have been targeted for violence as a result of the color of their skin, their sexual orientation, that is what this statute . . . is designed to cover. We don't have the indication that the attack was motivated by a person's desire to strike at somebody who was in one of these protected groups. That would not be covered by the statute"[1]

In other words, if you are a straight-white-Christian-man this bill does not protect you. This is an example of selective protection given through the use of hate crime laws and one of its many dangers. As this situation reveals, all hate crimes laws are prejudice. Their purpose is to protect one race against another, one religion against another, one gender against another, one sexual lifestyle against another. Holder himself went on to illustrate this point when he "stated that the murder of Army Private William Andrew Long in Little Rock, Arkansas would not be considered a hate crime, even though Private Long was killed by a black, Islamic convert that admitted to shooting Private Long simply because he was wearing an American uniform."[2]

Holder admits that there was "a certain element of hate," but the reason this hate bill will not cover Long is because "we're looking for here in terms of the expansion of the statute are instances where there is a historic basis to see groups of people who are singled out for violence perpetrated against them because of who they are. I don't know if we have the same historical record to say that members of our military have been targeted in the same way that people who are African- American, Hispanic, people who are Jewish, people who are gay, have been targeted over . . . the many years."[3]

Sadly, too many want to make such laws about sermons and personal beliefs, but really, in the end, it is about reverse prejudice.

---

1. Yount, "Hate Crimes Bill Will Not Provide Equality Before the Law According to US Attorney General," lines 14–18.

2. Ibid., lines 19–21. For more on the Private Long shooting, see Abrams, "Little Rock Shooting Suspect Joins Growing List of Muslim Converts Accused of Targeting U.S."

3. Yount, "Hate Crimes Bill Will Not Provide Equality Before the Law According to US Attorney General," 23–28.

Too many well-intentioned lawmakers feel that racial and sexual minorities have been considered outcasts and denied their rights for far too long and thus they seek to level the playing field. What they do, in the end, is punish prejudice by being prejudice. They raise the bar of equality by silencing out opposition. Did no one really not think about protecting the pastor in the above hypothetical? Is he not as worthy of protection as the homosexual? What about the Army private? Was he not worth the same protection as a minority? This is not an issue of sexual orientation, race, or religious belief but about the law's responsibility to show no favoritism. Justice is blind is it not?

But this is the danger of hate crime laws. Not only does it endanger Constitutional rights, but they are oftentimes used to protect some and not others. And if it selectively protects, it selectively threatens some and not others. Such laws do not ensure liberty, but only reverses prejudices.

As a Christian and a pastor this concerns me. This is not just about homosexuality but about anything that might be said in a public forum like a sermon. What if I preach a sermon on hell, or on the sinfulness of abortion, or on the corruption of the culture and the destruction of the family that offends someone? What if that someone is a minority? Suddenly I become a danger to society for simply professing my religious belief. Will the Bible now be considered a form of hate speech?

In the end, neither the pastor nor his sermon is put on trial but the faith of the pastor and his adherents. We become guilty by association. See the slippery slope? Already in other nations religious texts like the Bible are considered hate speech and is therefore a danger to society.[4]

---

4. Canada, for example, has passed bill C-250 into law which many believe will make various Biblical passages regarding the sinfulness of homosexuality hate speech or at the very least preaching from such texts as inciting hate. One example is Hugh Owens who was fined thousands of dollars for placing an ad that included two stickmen holding hands with a line through them with four Biblical texts to the left. The point of the add was to show that the Bible

The danger of such laws, and how Holder articulates them, sends us down a slippery slope in which there seems to be no return. The Constitution is under assault. Our nation finds itself following the footsteps of other Western nations who have used such laws as an excuse to prosecute and silence the Church. Any religious belief that stands contrary to the fickleness of the culture will be deemed as inappropriate and criminal. In the end, this is an attempt to silence some in the defense of others and with it democracy dies and prejudice, in reverse, is propagated.

Democracy and freedom can thrive only when dissenting voices are allowed to speak. Yes the shouts can at times offend, but to selectively protect one over another is nothing more than the sort of prejudice that we are seeking to overturn. Therefore, lawmakers should think twice before voting on a bill that would make them appear sensitive to the needs of minorities, while at the same time trample on the freedom of others.

Let freedom ring and let freedom sing . . . even if we get our feelings hurt every once in a while.

---

condemned homosexuality. Owens case was later repealed. However, the fact one was seriously fined for simply referencing Scriptures for inciting hate is frightful.

18

The Missing Gene

The Failed Search for the Gay Gene

HOMOSEXUALITY CONTINUES to be a divisive issue in America. Though a small percentage of Americans consider themselves gay, many have rallied behind their cause and fought for equal protection and rights. One common and key argument made by proponents of homosexuality is orientation meaning that homosexuality is not a choice but a birthright. If a gene can be found proving that sexual orientation is determined at birth, then one's sexual lifestyle is not only morally permissible, but also a civil right. With such a gene, homosexuality cannot be considered as an abomination against God, but rather a gift from God. Thus the gay gene would make homophobia as criminal as racism. Equating their cause with racial equality is a strategic way to legalize homosexuality.

Though the argument has promise there remains no evidence. Unless we make a "gay of the gaps" hypothesis, the argument remains ludicrous due to the absence of any evidence. Scientists like Francis Collins, a leading geneticist and the former head of the National Human Genome Research Project, simply concludes that homosexuality is "not hardwired by DNA."[1] And he is not alone.

---

1. Byrd, "'Homosexuality Is Not Hardwired,' Concludes Head of Human Genome Project," line 20.

Many scientists affirm that homosexuality is not predetermined by our genes.

The evidence is so lacking that even homosexual activists are admitting it. Peter Tatchell, a British gay activist, has admitted that there is no evidence whatsoever that the homosexual lifestyle is determined at conception. In fact, Tatchell finds the idea of a "gay gene" preposterous. He argues that sexuality is more "ambiguous, blurred, and overlapping than any theory of genetic causality can allow." One of the main problems with the gay gene argument is what Tatchell calls "sexual flexibility." If homosexuality is the result of "rigid erotic predestination," then what explains the common narrative of persons suddenly changing sexual lifestyles? There are countless men and women who marry into heterosexual relationships and have children who after years of marriage suddenly become homosexual.[2]

His argument is interesting. The fact that people suddenly change in the middle of their life does suggests that a gay gene does not exist. If we are hardwired toward a certain sex then it seems that mankind has done a very good job hiding it. The gay gene implies that there have been millions, if not billions, of persons born gay who have lived a heterosexual lifestyle their entire life and did not know they were actually hardwired gay.

Tatchell also distinguishes between genes that influence and genes that cause. Certainly there are a number of variables that may contribute to one's decision to practice homosexuality and oftentimes one's desire for the same sex can be quite strong. Strong enough to leave one feeling as if they were born that way. But to be influenced, nonetheless, means to make a choice. Everyone is influenced before making a choice, but a choice it remains. "Orientation," Tatchell says, "is still uncertain." The problem with the gene/orientation argument is that if it were true, "we would expect it to appear in the same proportions, and in similar forms, in all cultures and all epochs." And the fact that we do not suggests

---

2. Tatchell, "Homosexuality: It Isn't Natural," lines 2–3, 15, 17.

that the gay gene is a farce. Therefore, homosexuals must shift the blame of their desires to various influences that contribute to their sexuality. And since two persons can share the same experiences and yet differ on sexuality later in life only adds to the evidence that homosexuality remains a choice.[3]

This is not all. The slippery slope argument applies here as well. If the hopes of finding such a gene persists then scientists should begin looking for a transvestite gene, a pedophilia gene, a polygamy gene, a bestiality gene, and all the rest. If one is predestined to be homosexual, then it is logical to conclude that others are also predestined to be an alcoholic, a child molester, a criminal, a womanizer, or any other alternative or destructive lifestyle. By searching for genes as an excuse, man is weaseling his way out of responsibility for his own immoral choices. The search for the gay gene is only part of the equation. Homosexuals are not the only ones searching for an excuse. Any lifestyle, under such a trend, can now blame their actions and desires on their genes and thus escape blame or responsibility.

This whole debate illustrates how man will do whatever he can to excuse his sin. A gay gene, or any other gene, would make us victims of our biology rather than guilty rebels. The search for the gay gene is man's attempt to tell God its not their fault they are who they are, it is God's. When we can blame someone else (in this case our biology and thus God) suddenly we are free from any guilt or shame. And if we are born with a particular gene then to live out one's biology is not immoral, but natural. This is no different than what Adam and Eve did in the Garden in Genesis 3. Adam blamed Eve and Eve blamed the serpent for their rebellion and the trend continues today. Rather than confess our sin and turn from it, we seek to blame it on others, on our society, and now, on our genes. "It's not my fault," we say, "God made me this way" thus echoing the pattern of the Garden.

---

3. Ibid., lines 46, 48–49.

To live in a world enslaved to our perceived genes is to live in a world of slavery. Interestingly, those who advocate the gay gene do so for their own liberation, when in fact, they are searching for their own enslavement. If genes could be identified that prove that we are predestined towards homosexuality, depression, alcoholism, or sexual assault, then it seems that the culture gives us a pink slip of no hope. If all that we do is the result of our genes, then what hope do we have of breaking free from the bondage of such lifestyles? By assigning such actions and lifestyles to our genes, the culture makes us a slave to our genes.

This is not far from the picture of Scripture. Though Scripture never hints at such genetic causes for sin, it does paint the sinner as a slave. Jesus said that whoever commits sin is a slave of sin (John 8:35). Likewise, the Apostle Paul argued that we are the slave to whom we obey. If we obey our depraved nature, then we are slaves of sin (Romans 6:16). The gospel, he goes on to say, liberates us from such a slavery, freeing us from obeying its many lusts (Romans 6:22). While the world searches for slavery in the name of liberation, the gospel offers liberation apart from the slavery of sin.

Though Peter Tatchell presents a devastating argument from the perspective of a homosexual, we must not paint him as someone on the "religious right." As a homosexual activist, Tatchell affirms the morality of homosexuality and fights for equal rights for homosexuals. He is, however, tired of wasted arguments raised by like-minded people and the search for the gay gene is at the top of that list. Tatchell believes that society should embrace homosexuality, not because of our genes, but because homosexuals deserve the same rights as heterosexuals because both are equally human.

Though Tatchell and the gospel of Jesus Christ disagree on the morality of homosexuality, both can at least agree that there is no homosexual birthright. Gay gene proponents have been dealt a mortal wound from which they may never recover. Christians must remain steadfast knowing that God has declared His verdict and it is not up for debate no matter who or what man may blame their sinful lives on, even if they try to blame it on their Creator. The gospel offers the remedy to our sin whether it be homosexuality or something else. The gospel frees us from our enslavement. The culture and its search for biological validation seeks to keep us in our chains.

19

The Next Step

Is Polyamory the Next Sexual Movement?

What comes next? That is the question that will be inevitably answered after homosexuality is normalized. Opponents of same-sex marriage rightly raise the issue that homosexuality is not the last straw. As Christians, we understand that fallen man is not content with their sin. Sin in a fallen culture will only increase and fallen man will seek more ways to indulge the flesh. So, what is next? Polygamy? Lowering the age of consent? Bestiality?

How about Polyamory?

Polyamory is similar to polygamy, but does not involve marriage. It consists of multiple couples who interchange with other couples living with them in their sexual experience. It is non-monogamous sexuality involving sexual promiscuity with multiple partners. Polyamory could be the next stage in our obsession with unrestrained sex.

As was discussed in previous chapters, once marriage is redefined to allow homosexuals, it will not be long before persons are making their case for other sexual lifestyles. By dumbing down the meaning of marriage by introducing no-fault divorces and redefining marriage by including homosexuals, it will be inevitable that the culture will begin a new debate about a new form of sexuality. Polyamory seems to be next.

The Next Step

We are already seeing the first steps of polyamory in the form of serial monogamy. So many couples divorce and remarry only to divorce and remarry that monogamy seems out of the picture. On top of that, the rise of cohabitation only contributes to the difficulty. Such a trend has led many marriages to expect, embrace, and encourage adultery. CNN reports that "the practice of having romantic relationships with multiple people at the same time with the full knowledge and consent of all involved – has been getting a lot of attention." The primary reasons, as one polyamorous man put it, "We found the expectation that one person should be our everything seemed unrealistic given our day and age."[1]

The advantage of polyamory is that marriage is not necessary. One can be married and have multiple partners or they can simply have multiple partners without being married to anyone. Already in the West, many couples are practicing it outside of marriage. One female reader asked "The Ethicist" at the New York Times, for his advice on a polyamory mess; should they tell others about their practice of "ethical nonmonogamy." The reader mentions that though she is married, she also has a boyfriend and one day her housekeeper caught her in bed with her boyfriend, not her husband, and is wondering if she should explain to her housekeeper about their polyamorous practice. The advice from "The Ethicist" was to simply close the door next time she has sex with someone other than her husband.[2]

The presence of polyamory continues to gain speed, especially as the homosexual movement moves forward. Many have rightly argued that legalizing and normalizing homosexuality opens the doors to all other sexual lifestyles. Polyamory seems to be next. One of the primary reasons for this trend is that the same arguments made by gay activists can easily be applied to other sexual lifestyles like polyamory.

---

1. Pawlowski, "Mate Debate," lines 32–37.
2. Cohen, "Open the Marriage, Close the Door."

Dr. R. Albert Mohler, Jr., President of the Southern Baptist Theological Seminary, writes that "Once marriage is redefined to allow for same-sex unions, any determination to maintain legal prohibitions against polygamy will be seen as merely arbitrary."[3] And with such an arbitrary approach to the issue, the culture will give in and begin to defend and promote this next step in sexual liberation. When sex is involved, the culture will never say no. If homosexuals are given the right to practice their lifestyles in private, then how can we deny polyamorists the same right? If homosexuality is a civil right, why is polyamory not the same? If homosexuality is not wrong, how is polyamory wrong? You cannot legislate morality right? Who are you to tell polyamorists that they are sinners? If they love one another and it is consensual, who are we to tell them no?

A culture that redefines institutions like marriage will always be redefining it. The moral decay of the culture has already begun. That seems to be the only limit our culture currently allows when speaking about sex, marriage, and relationships.

We see then that issues like marriage, family, childbearing, and sexuality become rather relative terms in a society that has replaced absolute, final, and binding truth with privatization and tolerance. The Church needs to be prepared to fight against more than just homosexuality and divorce. Those are only the tip of the iceberg. As Christians, we must be armed with the gospel that transforms the soul and sanctifies the sinner. We are all sinners in need of being remade. As the culture continues to become more deviant, we must realize that the answer is not just elections, politics, and law, but the preaching of Christ and Him crucified. And as the Apostle Paul told us (Ephesians 5:25–26), let us model the cross in our marriages and save ourselves, our families, and our culture a world of hurt and immorality.

---

3. Mohler, "Polyamory—The Perfectly Plural Postmodern Condition," lines 19–21.

PART THREE

Politics: Where Reasonable Faith Meets Unreasonable Policy

20

Must Conservatives Believe in God?

The Role of God in Shaping Our Politics

Can one be both a conservative and an atheist? Does political, economic, moral, and foreign policy conservatism depend on one's view of God? At the popular conservative blog American Thinker, Shane Corsey argues that one can be conservative even without a fundamental belief in God. Corsey is case in point. He makes it clear that he does not believe in God and has serious objections to religion. He goes so far as to suggest that "God and religion do not belong in politics or . . . in the public arena."[1] One must ask if this is a consistent worldview? Can one hold to conservative values like small government, low taxes, healthy families, a strong national defense, free market capitalism, and be pro-life without any belief in God?

In a word, no. As Corsey lays out his argument, one is left wondering why Corsey is a conservative in the first place? On what foundation is conservatism based on without a fundamental belief in God? Corsey begins his argument by suggesting that conservatism is the "closest to the belief of what our Founding Fathers had in mind for this country, and the values of that system give an equal shake to anyone who wishes to come here. Religion in my

---

1. Corsey, "God, Conservatism, and Values," lines 12–14.

opinion is not as forgiving and can be as big of a divider in this country as race."[2]

But one must wonder, then, why follow the beliefs of the Founding Fathers? Why has he limited his political approach to that of the Founding Fathers and the Constitution? Why them? Furthermore, one must ask on what basis was America founded on? Being that Corsey's political standard was set by our Founders, one must further ask where did their ideas of life, liberty, and the pursuit of happiness originate? Certainly centuries of political theory and philosophy were behind much of the Founder's demand for liberty and a democratic republic, but the question remains, where did such fundamental convictions of the Founding Fathers come from? Where did the fundamental beliefs in human liberty and equality originate if not from God?

Though the Founding Fathers stopped short of pushing one particular religion or theology, their belief in the existence and providence of God stood as the foundation for their political thought. Even a cursory read of the founding documents and the Founding Fathers themselves affirms this conviction.[3]

Furthermore, no nation will establish a small government that promotes liberty instead of tyranny if it denies the authority and providence of God. We need to look no further than the 20th century for validation. The rise of atheistic regimes led to tyranny unlike any other. By rejecting God, government becomes the highest authority in the life of the people. Even in atheistic nations the people must follow and submit to someone and when God is denied, government willingly takes His empty seat (and His unlimited authority). The Founders opposed a federal religion for this very reason, but knowing, at the same time, that without a fundamental belief in God, the people would turn to the govern-

---

2. Ibid., lines 18–21.

3. There have been a number of books tracing the influence of Theism (and Deism) in our nation's founding. One good survey is Meacham, The American Gospel.

ment who would take away personal freedom. So long as equality and freedom originated from God, government had no power or right over its citizens.

Corsey raises an interesting point regarding the divisiveness of religion. Most religions, including Christianity, regards itself as the one true religion and rightfully so. Why bother with a religion if it offers no assurance or conviction? If one can find God anywhere, why bother participating in a particular religion? But we must not forget the serious questions that religion seeks to answer like how can one be made right with God? How can one escape judgment? What is the meaning of life? Why are we here? Is there a God? What is right and wrong? Even atheists have their own answers to these questions. At the same time we must not fall for the trap that says that religion is divisive while atheism is not. Anytime atheism gains in any society, it not only divides, but conquers. By bashing religion, Corsey shows that he is not free from the divisiveness he claims to be set apart from. Corsey ridicules religion in a divisive tone.

Corsey continues his argument by focusing primarily on the issue of homosexuality. To him, homosexuality is proof of the divisiveness of religion. He argues:

> Religion also leaves many people by the wayside if you don't subscribe to their beliefs. Many gays and lesbians share all the same values as any other American yet they are shunned in most religious circles, because of their sexual preferences. I'm a happily married man and I do not subscribe to their way of doing things, but who am I, or who are you, to judge them? . . . I also believe that they should be entitled to anything that a married couple should be entitled to, including adoption and getting the other spouse's Social Security benefits after one spouse has passed on.[4]

One can see where the fundamental difference between an atheistic and theological worldview lie. The issue of morality is itself divisive and the homosexual debate only adds fuel to the fire. From an atheistic worldview, there is no reason to regard homo-

---

4. Corsey, "God, Conservatism, and Values," lines 28–34.

sexuality wrong. Apart from a Divine Lawgiver why condemn two people in love, even if they are of the same sex?

But this raises an important issue regarding morality. Why does Corsey consider homosexuality to be moral yet other sexual preferences immoral? On what basis is he making his conclusions? Corsey goes on to raise the issue of the slippery slope: if homosexuality is permitted what about polygamy, polyamory, incest, or even bestiality? Can the same arguments in favor of homosexuality be made for these other lifestyles? And if so, then why deny polygamists their right to fulfill their own sexual desires?

Corsey allows this to be a possibility, but yet remains firm in his conviction that there should be limits to what the State considers sexually lawful. He says that as long as "gays and lesbians follow the same value system as the rest of us, are over the age of 18, are not accosting minors, and they are doing it of their own free will and not being forced into it, then they are not harming anyone, and should not be ridiculed or excluded from society or religion for that matter."[5] But why? On what grounds are his limits to sexuality based on? On what basis can one deny a minor and an adult, regardless of their genders, the right to participate in sexual activity? On what basis can one deny bisexual polygamy between adults and minors? Why must it be consensual? What do you mean by a shared "value system?" Must everyone line up with the same shared value system? If so, what value system? Can we really say we are democratic if everyone shared the same value system?

Apart from a fundamental belief in God who acts as a Divine Lawgiver that determines what is right and wrong, moral relativism is inevitable and as a culture evolves, so will its morality. One can easily rationalize immorality when God is absent. Can Corsey say today that if he were still alive one hundred years from now he would still limit marriage to just two persons regardless of genders? By then not only will homosexuality likely be legal and embraced, but so will other sexual lifestyles. On what basis does

5. Ibid., lines 36–39.

one draw limits and laws within a society when morality is relative on account of the absence of a holy deity? Such a philosophy leaves only the option of simply making up moral claims. Divorce and homosexuality were morally wrong one hundred years ago, but today it is not because society has said so and society has drawn such conclusions arbitrarily because of its rejection of God. Without definitive absolutes drawn from an immutable God, society is free to redefine all ethics and morality. What is wrong today might be right tomorrow.

Corsey goes on to provide more moral and political conclusions based on this weak foundation. He adds that neither sexual education (except "maybe in high school, but before that, it should be limited to discussions of the differences in gender only, and only with parents attendance"[6]) or prayer should be promoted in schools. Prayer promotes one religion over another and sexual education is abused and encourages students to violate possible moral convictions. In short, "School is for learning, not for teaching about sex or religion."[7]

Again, on what basis does Corsey make such conclusions? If homosexuality is a shared value among Americans why not teach and endorse it in public schools? If prayer is a shared value among Americans why not allow it in public schools? Corsey is again left determining policy out of a straw hat of his own design. True theism, on the other hand, cannot so conveniently determine morality on its own, but must submit to the moral character of God.

But perhaps the most amazing argument comes in the concluding paragraph. The atheist conservative argues:

> In values we can all find common ground, but not so much with religious views—too many differences. Right and wrong have no religion, they are of almost every religion and of none. Don't get me wrong, I think religion does have its place in our society, but that place is a place of our own choosing, not

---

6. Ibid., lines 44–46.
7. Ibid., line 50.

religion's choosing. Religion does not choose us, we choose whatever religion we choose to be. But American values and principles reside in the vast majority of all Americans, and can be used to bring all of us closer together regardless of religion, race, or sexual orientation.[8]

"Right and wrong have no religion?" His argument is that one cannot say that the morality of one's religion is superior to another religion (including non-religion) because all religions teach basically the same thing. This is simply not true. Already Corsey has shown his moral view regarding sexuality that runs contrary to many other religious beliefs. If God is not needed in conservatism then does that mean that Corsey's moral opinions rooted in his atheistic worldview become the standard that one must adopt in order to be included in the conservative movement? Is Corsey not encouraging his readers to follow him and not their religious beliefs that run contrary to his moral beliefs? Is that not divisive?

If conservatism does not need social conservatives then he has excluded millions of Americans from his club. That is the very definition of division. If Corsey seeks a broader tent where atheists, agnostics, and theists can work together to push an agenda based on common political, economical, and social beliefs, then fine. But already he is calling for the exclusion of religion. By making religion purely a private matter he is treating faith as an unwelcomed guess under the conservative tent. That conviction sounds more progressive than conservative.

If right and wrong have no religion then where does right and wrong originate? Neither atheism nor evolution can explain why all are innately born with a conscience and a sense of right and wrong. Morality originates with the Divine. By making the bold assertion that right and wrong do not originate in religion, Corsey is making a theological statement in which atheism is no match. The very existence of morality and the government pursuit of just laws is proof of God. No God demands anarchism where each

---

8. Ibid., lines 62–67.

individual becomes his own god determining his own rules. The only option atheism is left with is to place government upon God's throne and allow government to determine morality and laws, but to do so would violate everything that conservatism stands for.

Such naiveté is folly. American democracy is built on division and cannot thrive without it. The purpose of the Bill of Rights, which is built on the assumption of the existence of God, is to ensure that democracy will flourish. This does not mean that atheists are not welcome to participate in our democracy, but that one must understand that in order for the American experiment to succeed there must be a collective belief in a providential Deity that stands above the American people and her elected officials. The minute people are told what not to say or the press is told what not to report is the minute democracy dies. Unity is wonderful, but apart from uniformity (which quenches freedom and liberty) it is impossible. There is no such thing as a uniformed democratic, free society.

So must one believe in God in order to be conservative? Regarding some political issues, like foreign policy, perhaps not. But regarding the issues raised by Corsey, such as limited government and morality, unless one affirm a belief in the Divine it is hard to imagine how one could be a consistent conservative. The atheist conservative sounds more like an atheistic moderate (or even liberal) regarding moral issues than his theistic counterparts and fails to explain why he believes in the small government principles of the Founding Fathers if God does not exist. Atheism has traditionally bred tyranny because man is created to submit to some higher authority. Reject God and government immediately takes His place.

As Christians, we must not forget the effect that our theology plays in our politics and our moral outlook. If we are bound by Scripture, then relativism is an unwelcomed guest. Relativism is the offspring of secularism. So long as America affirms its traditional and founding belief in a providential God who stands as the ultimate judge over our actions, policies, and vote, then we will uphold the legacy and will of our Founding Fathers. But the minute we let go of such a foundation, then all that the Founders stood for will crumble before our very eyes.

God is fundamental to freedom, democracy, republic, and conservative values. We cannot have one without the other no matter how hard we might try.

21

The Lion of the Senate and the Lamb of God

The Pope, the Politician, and the Plea for Grace

THE DEATH of Senator Edward M. Kennedy marks the end of an era. For the first time in decades, a Kennedy does not occupy the Massachusetts Senate seat. Senator Kennedy was the last of the big three Kennedy brothers. Following the tragic deaths of President John F. Kennedy and his brother Robert, the mantle of the Kennedy name fell upon his shoulders. Of all of the Kennedy's, Edward will likely go down as the one who contributed the most to American history. Serving the public for half a century, Kennedy became known as the "Lion of the Senate" and influenced policy, presidents, and the direction of the country.

Prior to his death, Senator Kennedy, a life-long Catholic, sent a letter to Pope Benedict XVI via President Barack Obama. In the letter, Kennedy sought assurance that upon his death the Lion of the Senate would be present with the Lamb of God. Kennedy wrote:

> "I have been blessed to be part of a wonderful family. And both of my parents, particularly my mother, kept our Catholic faith at the center of our lives . . . I know that I have been an imperfect human being, but with the help of my faith, I have tried to right my path.
>
> I want you to know, Your Holiness, that in my nearly 50 years of elective office, I have done my best to champion the rights of the poor and open doors of economic opportunity. I have worked to welcome the immigrant, to fight discrimina-

tion and expand access to health care and education. I have opposed the death penalty and fought to end war."[1]

The late Senator went on to add that he has also fought for health care for everyone in America. He continues to trust that his colleagues in the Senate would continue to fight for "the political cause" of his life and everyone would indeed have equal access to health care.

He concluded: "I have always tried to be a faithful Catholic, Your Holiness, and though I have fallen short through human failings, I have never failed to believe and respect the fundamental teachings of my faith. I continue to pray for God's blessings on you and on our church and would be most thankful for your prayers for me."[2] Kennedy's plea is understandable. Those who lie dying want the assurance that God will accept their soul into heaven. Though Kennedy was powerful, he could not overcome the certainty of death and his accountability in the next life. In Kennedy's letter one theme runs through: has he done enough to gain the favor of God Almighty?

In answer to that question Kennedy points to a number of accomplishments and good works in his life (most of them political). He turned to his Catholic faith in moments of great difficulty and tragedy. Throughout his life, he tried to right his path and override his personal failings with good works. He had defended the poor and needy. He opened doors to economic justice. He welcomed immigrants without discrimination. He fought against the death penalty and unjust wars. Finally, Kennedy had fought vehemently to grant health care for everyone.

Kennedy certainly fought for a lot of causes in his public career. There are no lies and no stretching the truth in this list of "accomplishments." But what affect did any of it have on his salvation? Will these things be enough to assure his entrance into the Kingdom of God? Sadly, Kennedy was looking for assurance in the

1. "Kennedy's Letter to the Pope," lines 9–16.
2. Ibid., lines 16–18.

wrong place. The Pope's brief reply is interesting. He never gave Kennedy the assurance he craved, but instead called on the Senator to surrender himself to the merciful will of God in faith trusting in His precious grace. Despite his many political causes, the Pope refused to promise the assurance Kennedy wanted the most.

Kennedy trusted his politics, while the Pope pointed to God's grace. Kennedy foolishly bought into the notion that somehow our good can outweigh our bad even though all that we do is tainted with sin including our good works. Do we really expect God to accept polluted righteousness?

The folly of Kennedy is a lesson that all need to learn. Not only are we to embrace the message of the cross, which says we are all sinners separated by God and yet can be reunited with Him in repentance, but we also ought to avoid the folly of equating our politics with the gospel. At the end of the day, Kennedy had no other source of assurance than his politics. In his letter to the Pope he says nothing about the cross, Christ, or the Resurrection, nor does he mention repentance or reflect a Biblical understanding of sin. Kennedy just had his politics. Sadly, many in America are falling into the same trap. When reflecting on what assurance we have after death, we recall a long list of good works; we never got divorced and we always voted for the right candidate. Sadly, we put more trust in our many good works than in Christ's one perfect work. Politicians and citizens alike believe that if only they support the right causes, donate to the right charities, or practice the right morality, God will take notice and overlook their fallen nature.

Kennedy's plea for salvation should humble us all. If the Pope could not grant the assurance he desperately craved, how much more us? Very few of us will have the political resume of the late Senator and yet we all foolishly believe that somehow we are still on God's good side. If this lion feared meeting the Lamb, how much more ought we? Kennedy was no perfect politician and seemed to always be involved in controversy, but at the end of his life, he was being humbled before the Lord he was about to meet.

But if we learn anything, let us learn that politics is no source of hope. Government has its role and Christians are called to submit to their leaders, but even the most powerful politicians can pass no legislation that would grant them what we all crave the most: assurance of salvation when this life gives way to the next. Kennedy fought as hard as anyone to please God, but apart from repentance, no politician or policy can redeem anyone and grant the hope of ever hearing, "Well done, good and faithful slave . . . Enter into the joy of your Master" (Matthew 25:23).

Christians must not fall for the folly that politics can replace theology. Kennedy's letter should remind us that at the end of the day, God is greater than any politician. Therefore, let us be about the business of the gospel and not so distracted with the business of government. Repentance is our only hope, not our voting record.

22

The Transcendence of Greed

What Economics Can Teach Us About the Gospel

CURRENT POLITICAL events and debates, particularly regarding the economy, healthcare, natural disasters, and public policy has only encouraged more divisive barking between liberals and conservatives in America. During a recent radio show an argument brewed between the host (a small government, fiscal conservative) and a caller (an economic liberal) over taxes, the rich, and the economy. Both made the same argument that has been repeated over and over again.

Liberals who lean towards a more socialistic model believe that rich people are greedy and evil and should be punished. For the sake of the whole nation, their excess should be taken and given to those less fortunate. They believe that capitalists are greedy and government should regulate the market in order to "look out for the little guy." On the other end of the spectrum, conservatives lean towards a more free-market model and believe that everyone is in charge of their own destiny. They charge that liberals and socialists hate and stand in the way of freedom. Government robs ingenuity and liberty, they say. Government is the problem. The smaller the government, the better the economy.

From the Christian perspective, both are right, but not in the way one might think.

The primary charge raised by the liberal was that conservatives and capitalists are greedy. They are exactly right. Adam Smith, the intellectual founder of capitalism, would agree with this. Smith understood that men were by nature greedy and thus developed his economic theory of capitalism on that doctrine. Both the customer and the businessman are greedy. The entrepreneur wants the customers money. The customer wants the best products for the cheapest price. They both contribute to the other's selfishness thus satisfying the greed of the other.

This is really the beauty of the capitalist system. Anyone who criticizes capitalism based on its lust for more money and power misses the point. Of course entrepreneurs want more money, that is why they are in business. They run their advertisements and decorate their businesses for the sole purpose of making more money. So to charge capitalism for being a system of greed is to only state the obvious. It was built and has thrived on it. This is why capitalism has brought economic prosperity in ways that no other economic theory has yet to produce. The rapid growth and power of the American economy in its short history is testament to it.

But socialist leaning liberals need to be careful; their economic theory is also guilty of greed. Socialism says, "it's not fair that I do not have what they have, therefore, what they have should be taken." That is greed. President Obama illustrated this well when he told Joe the Plumber on the campaign trail that he wanted to take his wealth and give it to others. That is greed. Capitalism is built on selfishness and socialism is built on theft. Socialism believes that the government should have authority over one's salary and economic prosperity. It will decide if someone makes too much, has too much, or should pay more in taxes. Whenever the government introduces a new program or runs a program into bankruptcy, instead of making tough decisions, it simply takes (or steals) from the rich and uses class envy as a means of justifying themselves. Many liberals find themselves saying things like, "the rich have more than they need; its not fair that they have so much while everyone else has so little." That is greed.

The Transcendence of Greed

Greed permeates both economic theories. Should we really be surprised by this? Whether one is a socialist, a communist, a Marxist, a capitalist, a conservative, a libertarian, or even an anarchist, all are stained with greed. This is precisely what the Christian worldview teaches; all of us are selfish and greedy; all of us want more for less work; all of us want what others have and will stop at no lengths of getting it. This is why the last commandment regards coveting and Jesus spoke so much about serving instead of being served (Matthew 20:28).

We are all greedy. The problem with these economic systems is not their theories (though both could be rightly criticized), but with human nature. It's not our economy that is sick, we are sick. So long as government and pundits run around trying to fix the exterior (like the economy or healthcare) nothing will be resolved. What we need is revival, not more or less taxes.[1]

Though government plays a vital role in society, more or less government is not the solution nor the debate that should occupy our time. The gospel is the solution. Greed can only be conquered by the cross, not through economic or tax policy. So long as everyone trusts in the decisions and programs (or the lack there-of) of government, the more divided and desperate we will be. Not until we become transformed by the gospel can real change be experienced.

Though we might shout and yell at one another over critical issues like the economy, let us not forget the most important issue: the external greed of man will not be remedied apart from the internal work of the Spirit. That is one thing both liberals and conservatives have taught us. We are all greedy and we all need the sort of change that cannot be brought about by government, but only by God.

Greed transcends all political and economic theories and policies, but so does the gospel, and thus why we must be about the business of evangelism. That is the sort of change we should all believe in.

---

1. Taxes themselves are based on greed. We want lower taxes so that we can keep more of our own money, yet at the same time, we think others should be taxed more so we can enjoy their wealth.

23

What Is to Be Our Response?

Living as a Christian in an Obama Administration

THE ELECTION of Barack Obama is both historic and controversial and any time new leadership is inaugurated, Christians must ask themselves how they are to respond and interact with the new administration. The truth is President Barack Obama will oppose most of what social conservatives and Christians stand for, most notably the protection of marriage and the sanctity of life. The Bible clearly lays out how Christians are to live as citizens regardless of who occupies the Whitehouse. It is imperative for believers to engage, interact, pray, and carefully articulate the Christian worldview regardless of who is elected to public office. Too often Christians treat a politician or a President with greater or lesser respect based on his party affiliation or convictions forgetting that God is not limited to a political party.

Let us not forget that God is sovereign over all, including governments, policy, law, and presidents. God can use both godly kings like David and pagan kings like Cyrus to fulfill His good will. By being too partisan many Christians confuse the gospel with politics. In order to prevent such a danger, we must search the Scriptures and see what they command us in light of new change and new directions for our country.

PRAYER

The first and primary response Christians should have is to pray. Paul wrote to Timothy that we should offer up "entreaties and prayers, petitions and thanksgivings,. . . [for] all men, for kings and all who are in authority, so that we may lead a tranquil and quiet life in all godliness and dignity" (1 Timothy 2:1-2). Though the command is clear, too many Christians fail to take the time and make supplication in behalf of their elected leaders. Unfortunately, when "our guy," is in office, we give thanks to God for helping him win the election, but once a politician we do not like is in power, we pray for his defeat and pray that "our party" will be able to defeat any legislation or policy he may put forward.

Paul draws no partisan line in his exhortation to pray. We must pray for our leaders in order "that we may lead a transquil and quiet life in all godliness and reverence," thus requiring us to pray for a number of particular things regardless of our leaders' party or convictions.

First, we must pray for our leaders to lead in godly wisdom like King Solomon. What we need from our leaders is not more partisan politics, but godly, wise leadership. Too often, politicians lead in a way that will insure their reelection rather than doing what is right for those they lead and for their country. Pray that God would open the eyes of our leaders to make right decisions for their country, not just for their prospects for reelection or for their own party. Wise leadership will lead to a more moral nation, stronger families, a safer and more secure nation, and justice for all regardless of sex, race, socio-economic status, or party affiliation.

Secondly, we must give thanks that God has raised up our leaders for this moment. Trusting in God's sovereignty means that God is not surprised by elections. God raises up leaders, we do not. This does not mean that elections do not matter or that we should refrain from voting, but that we should not act as if God has let us down because "our guy," was not elected. God raises up leaders and uses them for His own purposes. Therefore, rather than complain to God about our officials, be grateful for them. Remember, God used the pagan king Cyrus though he was godless and not Republican. Giving thanks always reminds us of God's Sovereignty, giving us the comfort in knowing that He is on His throne regardless of any mess coming out of Washington.

Thirdly, we must pray for the safety and prosperity of our officials and the nation they lead. Our nation is in constant threat. Let us pray, regardless of party affiliation, that God will protect our nation from another national tragedy and attack. We must pray that God, in His sovereignty and wisdom, prosper our leaders for the sake of those they lead and protect them from any danger that may befall them or our country.

Furthermore, we must pray for peace. Though we live in a fallen world, we must seek to be peacemakers and pray that our leaders will bring about peace, not war. This does not mean that war is never justified, but where available we should seek reconciliation and peace over military action and war. This means that Christians should be as active in bringing about peace as politicians. We have the true gospel given to us by the Prince of Peace and no diplomat or foreign policy council will bring the sort of peace that the gospel can bring. Pray that God grants us peace even in this depraved, fallen world.

Finally, pray for the furtherance of the gospel. Our main priority is the gospel, not politics. We seek men to repent before God, not for different voting habits. Certainly our votes say a lot about our convictions and our understanding of what it means to be a Christian, but our priority must be on the gospel. The gospel drives our politics; our politics do not drive the gospel. We do not seek to make the nation Republican or Democrat, but to see God glorified through the salvation of souls. We pray that our leaders will allow the gospel to go forward instead of standing in its way.

This is only a short list of things to consider when praying for leaders. More could be added. It is necessary, nonetheless, to consistently and wholeheartedly pray for our political leaders regardless of their party. We seek something greater than the next election; we seek God's glory and in His Sovereignty, God has given us governments to keep the peace and to contain sin. In the meantime, let us seek for the gospel to move forward, and our leaders to submit to their Maker and lead their nation in a godly manner.

SUBMISSION

Paul also commands us to submit to government (Rom. 13). This is easier to do when a pro-life, pro-traditional marriage, openly Christian President occupies the White House but what about a president with whom we have very little in common, especially on issues we dare not compromise on?

First, we must be reminded that Jesus, Paul, and all of the first Christians never had a political leader that agreed with them on anything. The government during their time repeatedly tried to stamp out the young, vibrant Church. Yet, rather than cry, "Woe is me!" they dropped to their knees and prayed and then submitted to the will of Caesar unless they were being coerced to abandon their faith.

As Christians, we are called to submit to the demands of government even when we disagree with them (in regards to policy). If taxes are raised, we must pay them. If laws are passed, we must obey them because God, in His sovereign and providential care, has given us our President whether we like it or not. Truth is, God could not care less what we think or what political party is in power. God is neither Republican, Democrat, nor Independent. He has given us our President and our elected leaders despite our protest or support. Submission to government is not a political issue, but an obedience issue.

One point needs to be made clear. Christians are called to submit to God before any other person or institution. This means that when God and government disagree, we must submit to God over the government. Therefore, we must not submit or obey whenever government demands we do something that God has commanded us not to do. Furthermore, we must not submit or obey when the government demands we do not do something God has commanded us to do.[1]

Scripture gives us a number of instances where believers did not obey the government (cf. Daniel, Shadrach, Meshach, and Abednego, and Peter and John). However, we must not be falsely looking for occasions to disobey simply because we disagree with a particular policy. Submission characterizes the Christian life. If God has established an institution (like government), then Christians are to submit to it, reflecting their submission to their Redeemer.

ENGAGEMENT

Finally, we must be willing to engage our elected officials with a gospel worldview. We are called to hold our government accountable, celebrate when they are right, correct them when they are wrong and doing so with an attitude of love, grace, compassion, concern, and conviction. We want the gospel to go forth and God glorified above all.

This is perhaps the toughest part of being a Christian in a fallen culture. It is tempting to believe that with the right politicians, policies, and laws we can win the "culture wars." We must not forget, however, that the problem with every nation is not just its policies and politicians, but with human nature. We must not put all of our trust in the institutions of man, but in the power of God and His gospel. We are called to be light who place our trust in the gospel first. Politics is always secondary. Oftentimes we confuse the two or at least blend them. Too often we fall for the

---

1. See MacArthur, "The Christian's Responsibility to Government – Part 1," lines 190–91.

trap of beginning with politics, thinking that it will bring about the spreading of the gospel. Christianity does have political implications, as do all worldviews, but we must begin with the heart of the sinner, not the tax policies of the Ways and Means committee.

Christians must remember that the Kingdom of God will not be realized by an election or through legislation, but through the spreading of the gospel. Jesus never ran for office and Paul never protested Roman policy. Our calling is not politics, but the gospel. True hope and change for a better future is not in a political Messiah, but in the One and True Messiah, Maker of heaven and Earth, who redeemed us at the cross.

Engaging the culture involves remaining informed about purposed bills, political philosophy, and current events and debates all while understanding where Christian theology meets public policy. This means that Christians must make an effort to be informed from more than conspiratorial emails and bias media reporting. Engaging the culture and the government is an everyday process that involves time and careful analysis and as we do, let us remember we must not take the gospel out of the equation. The Christian worldview must always be at the forefront of how we view the world and those who lead it. In order to engage we must be informed by both the world in which we live and the gospel in which we proclaim and live by.

CONCLUSION

At the start of every new election cycle, let us act as Christians, not as angry Republicans, Democrats, Libertarians, or Independents. We seek to fulfill the Great Commission to the glory of our Savior. Our hope is in the triumph of the foolishness of the cross (1 Corinthians 1:18-31), not in the wisdom of Congress or pundits.

The Great Commission will never be thwarted or promoted by a politician, but will only be fulfilled by the Spirit of God. We should care and be passionate about saving the meaning of marriage and the lives of the innocent, but more importantly, we should be focused on saving the souls of men and women with the gospel of Jesus Christ. No political or legal ground will be gained unless the hearts and minds of men and women are turned from sin and towards the cross. The gospel is our first priority as we submit to the will of our Father and obey His every command. How we interact, engage, and elect our leaders says a lot about our convictions. Let us live in the public sphere reflecting a more biblical worldview, centered on the gospel, free from partisan bickering. That is the sort of change I can believe in.

24

Prophet, Priest, and President

Is Obama Really the Messiah?

DURING THE 2008 Presidential campaign, many conservatives frequently pointed out the cult-like following of now President Barack Obama from his supporters. Stories and video of persons fainting when he appeared and spoke were common and even Obama himself joked that he was not born of a virgin despite what many may think. The mainstream media only encouraged it by making it appear Obama had a halo over his head like a saint or an angel. Obama was frequently viewed as the candidate that would save Washington, America, and the world. Many saw Obama as the answer to their prayers. Hope and change had finally come to Washington.

Now, long after his inauguration, the madness has yet to end. In an interview, Newsweek's Evan Thomas referred to Obama as a "sort of god" who is "standing above the country," and "above the world."[1] Thomas has since said that his words were taken out of context, and he should be given the benefit of the doubt.[2] I seriously doubt that Thomas considers Obama as some sort of literal

1. Matthews, "'Hardball with Chris Matthews' for Friday, June 5," lines 253–54.

2. After admitting to having put his foot in his mouth, Thomas wrote, "I was not being literal. During a discussion about presidential rhetoric, I was comparing Ronald Reagan's patriotic appeals with Obama's attempt to transcend—parochialism." Thomas, "The Perils of Punditry," lines 13–15.

LOGIZOMAI

god, but at the same time, this is not the first time we have seen someone, particularly in the media, consider Obama as the greatest politician and hope America has seen (Thomas said this while on Hardball with Chris Matthews who himself has said that the coming of Obama is like the coming of the New Testament[3]).

As an American, I cannot help but laugh. Why would anyone elevate a politician to such status? But every election we fall for this same trap. Politicians promise to fix our taxes, lower the cost of health care, fix the economy, and bring world peace and so we elect them thinking that they will solve all of our problems, and, when they do not, we complain and elect the next politician who makes the same promises. Certainly some elections carry this tendency more than others, but after eight controversial years of the Bush administration, many Americans were looking for someone quite different. And at that moment, a Senator from Chicago, with good speaking skills and great charisma, announced that he was running for the nation's highest office.

Every politician has his own constituency and every politician has let that constituency down. Just as former President George W. Bush disappointed fiscal conservatives, President Obama has disappointed the anti-war and the gay community down. Yet in spite of the constant disappointment, Americans continue to put their trust in any politician that says the right things and makes the right promises. In a nation built on liberty and small government, we are quick to believe the empty promises coming from every campaign trail. Have we not learned our lesson?

But as a Christian, I am more concerned. Too many Christians have put their trust in politicians rather than in their God and Savior. Both liberals and conservatives are guilty of this. We have substituted tax reform or new education legislation for the gospel and like our non-believing counterparts, we have bought into the notion that all will be well if only our guy wins.

---

3. Gillette, "Primary Scream," lines 36–38.

This does not mean that Christians should not vote or get involved in politics. One should be very much engaged in politics, following cultural trends, ethics, and debate. However, Christians must not foolishly believe that somehow the Church will grow, people will be saved, or that the Kingdom of God (both present and future) will be realized as long as the guy or party they like is in power.

Although many believe otherwise, Jesus in the Gospels could not have cared less about the politics of His day. He had one mission: to save the lost by shepherding them to the cross. Jesus never fought for social reform or suggested government solutions to anyone's problems. Everything He did and said was about the cross. It is at the cross that man finds hope and answers, not Washington or Rome.

To put our trust in a politician or a political party is a form of idolatry. Israel wanted a king, but God had His reservations because God Himself was their King. By asking for a king, the people were revealing their true hearts: they wished to dethrone God and replace Him with one of their own. Furthermore, God knew that once the people had a king, they would look to the king for hope and answers, not God. This does not mean that the Jews ceased worshiping God, but instead of trusting in God, they first put their trust in the king.

The same happened during Jesus' time. John 6 records the feeding of the five thousand whereby the people responded by trying to force Jesus into becoming their king. They believed that if Jesus were their political king, then they would never have to work for food again. To them, Jesus could fulfill their Utopian dream and so rather than embrace the message of the gospel, the people sought to force him to become a king. The people wanted a savior, but the wrong kind of savior.

Every nation has fallen into this trap. Whenever the people start putting their trust in a politician instead of the Creator, disappointment and folly are around the corner. In the end, Obama will be a disappointment. He might go down as a great President, but he will not succeed in fulfilling the desires of those who elected him. Obama will inevitably not be the President he has allowed himself to be portrayed as during the campaign. Obama has allowed the perception that once he got elected, peace would come, poverty would end, and all will be made new. By allowing this perception to go on, Obama has set himself up for a huge fall.

Obama is no messiah. He is no savior. He is no "sort of god." He is an elected leader chosen to fulfill a task to the best of his ability. He is human and will make many mistakes. As Christians, it is time for us to be gospel-centered rather than politics-centered; Christ-centered rather than man centered. The world will not be saved through a President or through politics but only when we preach the gospel to every soul and trust in the sanctifying work of the Holy Spirit regardless of what may happen in Washington or who may occupy its highest office.

25

The Real Solution to Global Warming

Human Extinction

EVERY THEOLOGY has its own Eschatology, or belief regarding the end times. Christians affirm the bodily return of Christ as prophesied throughout Scripture and described in the book of Revelation. Secularists have their own eschatology: climate change. Based on the imminent return of Christ, Christians are commanded to call on men everywhere to repent of their sins before it is too late. Likewise, secular eschatology warns of certain apocalyptic disaster that can only be curbed by repenting of our ecological sins. Just as much Christian apocalyptic imagery involves judgment, death, and chaos, so does the secular apocalypse. Global warming, it is said, will leave much of the world underwater due to the melting of the polar ice caps; it is also blamed for natural disasters, increase sun damage, and even blamed for shrinking sheep. One cannot miss the many similarities between religious eschatologies and global warming. Again, everyone is a theologian.

Global warming is a popular issue these days and has morphed into almost an exclusively political one. The leading face of the global warming movement is without a doubt former Vice-President Al Gore, whose books and documentary have impacted millions around the world and even won him a Nobel Peace prize. Due to the political climate of the movement it is virtually impossible to separate climate change from political action and government intrusion.

Every hurricane, tsunami, or winter storm is almost always blamed on global warming and used as a catalyst for climate change legislation as proponents warn that "the end is near."

Despite the urgency of many alarmists the theory has a number of problems. Its scientific evidence is not as consensual as previously lauded and the data used to support the theory has been called into doubt in light of recent allegations of scientists exaggerating data. Furthermore, scientists seem uncertain as to if the earth is cooling or warming. Currently the popular trend leans towards warming, but in previous decades scientists warned of the coming ice age. But there is a more fundamental problem. Even if global warming is happening and is the fault of human activity, the exact solution remains a mystery. Governments, politicians, and activists have all proposed their own solution: passing a carbon tax, banning global warming causing light bulbs and appliances, driving fuel efficient cars, and buying a water filter instead of bottled water. However, if the truth be told and the scientists, activists, and governments were honest, these proposed solutions are not enough. No amount of solar panels or wind turbines will curb human cause global warming or prevent the inevitable apocalypse from happening. Small changes are not enough. Therefore, a growing number of global warming alarmists are concluding that the only hope we have for saving the planet from apocalyptic destruction is extinction. The group is called the Voluntary Human Extinction Movement (VHEM) and they propose that humans must cease reproducing in order to save the planet from human caused global warming.[1] How they will succeed remains unseen, certainly abortion and other forced sterilization methods must be enforced, but unless sterility becomes mandatory, the movement will gain no traction.

But the VHEM might be on to something. The secular left's distortion of marriage and family has caused the culture to inad-

---

1. Their slogan is "May we live long and die out" as seen on their home page at http://www.vhemt.org/.

The Real Solution to Global Warming

vertently practice this. The average European home, for example, consists of one child.[2]

It does not take long for such a culture to meets its end or to be replaced by immigration. So the idea of a sterile culture, though seemingly improbable, could theoretically happen apart from any religious and moral convictions which secular societies work hard on eradicating.

But history and common sense have shown that extinction movements always become, well, extinct. The Shakers, for example, were a group of Protestants who abstained from sex even among married couples and thus died out in a very short time. Sterility led to their demise. If we have learned anything from them, and others like them, it is that any sterile movement will die while the human race will only continue. And it is the entire race of homosapians that VHEM seeks to destroy.

To put it simply, it is a waste of time. Alarmists have been hinting at this solution for years now and the truth is that changing light bulbs, driving hybrids, and taking shorter showers will do nothing to end human caused global warming. The only logical answer to this "problem" is for those guilty of causing global warming (humans) to cease to exist.

However, even this solution to the apocalyptic theory will not end global warming as it is currently promoted. Though cars, factories, and carbon-emitting humans might be gone, animals and plants will be left behind who themselves contribute to climate change. Animals such as moose and cattle are adding to the crisis "by burping, belching and excreting copious amounts of methane" in the air. Such animals have been blamed for emitting more CO_2 than cars. [3]

---

2. Global Envision reports, "In many countries, such as Czech Republic, Germany, Greece, Italy, Poland, the Russian Federation, Spain and Ukraine, fertility levels are now closer to one child than two children per couple," in Joseph Chamie, "Fewer Babies Pose Difficult Challenges for Europe," lines 41-43.

3. Singh, "Cows with Gas: India's Global Warming Problem," lines 9-10.

If we are gone, both cows and moose (and other animals) will destroy the planet. The eradication of humans will only lead to a higher population of animals who themselves have contributed to the problem. Global warming, it seems, is not just human caused, but also animal caused. If extinction of the human race is the only solution, then we better remove the animal kingdom first.

And it does not stop there. Even if every human and animal were eliminated, the world would still not be saved from global warming. According to some scientists, not only are humans and animals contributing to global warming, but so are plants.[4] That means that purchasing carbon offsets (which many compare to doing penance) actually contributes to global warming rather than offsetting one's carbon footprint. If plants produce global warming then planting trees should only add to the problem.

So will the VHEM proposal work? Not unless they intend on sterilizing all humans, animals, and plants since it seems like everything but rocks and dirt contribute to global warming. If extinction is our only hope, then we must leave the earth quite bare. Of course this will never happen due to opposition from animal and plant rights activists.

The VHEM, however, do deserve some respect. Global warming deniers raise the issue of government control. They argue that global warming is more about politics than actual science. The recent "climategate" scandal has only added fuel to the fire. As the controversy continues to unravel, it has been revealed that some scientists exaggerated some of the data in order to get politicians to act more urgently. Politics, it seems, did overshadow some of the science. In addition, the proposed solutions to prevent catastrophic global warming (which involve changing our light bulbs,

---

See also Lean, "Cow 'Emissions' More Damaging to Planet Than CO2 Cars.

4. Jha, "Global Warming: Blame the Forests." The article begins, "They have long been thought of as the antidote to harmful greenhouse gases, sufferers of, rather than contributors to, the effects of global warming. But in a startling discovery, scientists have realised that plants are part of the problem," lines 1–4.

getting fuel efficient cars, painting our roofs and roads white, recycling, unplugging appliances when not in use, turning one's thermostat down and water heater off while absent, taking shorter baths, or a host of other solutions) are futile. This can only mean that the VHEM is right; the only solution to global warming is the complete annihilation of all life on earth. So long as life exists, the environment remains in danger.

But extinction of life does not necessarily mean the end of all life. According to another popular scientific theory, the Earth consisted of inorganic objects and somehow, through the process of mutations and chance taking place over millions of years, life was "born." Rocks and mud gave way to life millions of years ago and through the survival of the species, man was able to reach the top of the food chain. If evolution happened once, maybe it will happen again only this time there will be no need for a big bang. We will leave behind a pristine earth ripe for life.

If there is no ultimate meaning or purpose in life, as evolution and secularism implies, then the planet is all that there is. Government is our god and nature is our sanctuary. Preserving the planet for future generations seems to be a moral cause in a world without certainty or purpose. Mother Earth is worth it, is she not?

The secular worldview inevitably leads down such unconscionable paths. Death is a necessary process for the thriving of future generations. Global warming is about more than just saving the planet, but about forfeiting our freedom for something bigger than us. Since God is no longer allowed in the public square, man must turn to other causes to live, and die, for. The likelihood of universal voluntary extinction is improbable at best, but the cause of the VHEM should not be ignored. Secularism breeds this sort of lunacy. Bad theology leads to horrendous ideas and organizations, like the Voluntary Human Extinction movement, which did not appear out of a vacuum.

Christians should be careful when it comes to the controversial issue of climate change. We affirm the sovereignty of Almighty God, Maker of Heaven and Earth. As Creator and Sustainer, every environmental catastrophe is within His control. This does not mean that Christians should be passive or lazy when it comes to stewardship, but to not be quick to buy into secular Apocalyptic scenarios. God has already written the last chapter of earth's history and in the meantime, let us be faithful stewards of God's creation, but not distracted by it. We must be about the business of the gospel. Forfeiting freedom and evangelism for an unproven scientific theory should give us reason to pause. We should take care of the planet, but that is not our main priority. Our first priority is to save those who dwell on Mother Earth, and as we do, let us be faithful stewards of the many gifts God has given us, including the environment. And we can do so without the heavy hand of Washington or without chasing unproven theories with radical implications.

Conclusion

EVERYONE HAS their own unique item they have preserved over the years. My wife has preserved the flowers I gave her when I proposed to her. Now, years later, she can open up our small scrap book and look at those flowers and be reminded of the day we got engaged. The flowers still look as good as they did then to this day. I, on the other hand, have dirt. While on a mission trip in Niger, Africa I collected some dirt from the village we were evangelizing in. It serves as a constant reminder of the necessity of missions and to pray for those on the front lines of carrying the gospel to unreached people groups.

I'm sure we all have our own peculiar things we have preserved. Maybe its hand prints from when the kids were young, a certain picture, an old baseball card, a signed poster, a letter, a souvenir, or something else. We all have them. Behind every one of them is a story we like to tell. What we preserve is what is most valuable to us. None of us preserve trash or a McDonald's wrapper because it has no inherent value to us. But we will preserve dirt from Africa or handprints from our children because they have a certain value to them. My wife has received a lot of flowers over the years, and yet she has never taken the time to preserve them. They have all died. Only those given to her the day we got engaged were given the value to be carefully preserved. What we preserve we value the most.

How many of us value the gospel and thus are careful to preserve it? Throughout her two thousand year history, the Church of Jesus Christ has all too often abandoned, redefined, or stripped down the gospel in order to make it more relevant, popular, or less offensive. The reason for such major errors is because the gospel has little or no value to us. We preserve only what we value the most.

During modernity, Christians began to strip the gospel of its supernatural elements. Gone were the Virgin Birth, a literal interpretation of Creation, miracles, and the resurrection. Never mind the Bible's clear teaching that unless Christ was raised from the dead, we remain in our sins (1 Corinthians 15:17) many Christians stripped the gospel of its supernatural and historical context in order to appear more relevant in an age of science and anti-supernaturalism. The rise of Protestant liberalism has been a cancer to the gospel. Rather than being united under the banner of a transcendent gospel, the Church has had to fight on two fronts: Protestant Liberals and the lost. When many abandon the gospel, true Christians are forced to clarify what the gospel actually is in contrast to those who claim to be updated, more relevant Christians.

Likewise, postmodernity has also encouraged Christians to abandon or at least strip down the gospel so that it will seem more relevant and user-friendly. Postmodernity's abuse of tolerance and open-mindedness has forced many Christians to deny doctrines like Hell, God's wrath, final judgment, and the gospel's exclusivity. The gospel is not good news if there is no bad news. In an attempt to appear loving and non-divisive, many have rejected the need for divisive doctrines and turned the message of Christ into humanitarian aide. Certainly the gospel commands us to care for the poor and to fight against injustice (see Matthew 25:40), but the priority of the gospel is to call on men everywhere to repent less they be destroyed by God. By ignoring the offensiveness of the cross, postmodern liberalism only encourages sin and rebellion against God.

Jesus calls us the "salt of the earth" (Matthew 5:13). One of the many uses of salt in the first century was that of a preservative. Christ is calling on His followers to preserve the gospel regardless of how offended others might be or how irrelevant to the culture it might seem. The immediate context of Jesus' words is interesting.

Prior to calling His believers salt, Jesus explains that His followers will be harassed and hated for His name sake as were the prophets beforehand (Matthew 5:10-12). Jesus is clear; the gospel is offensive and many will not stand for it. But rather than feel sorry for ourselves, Jesus calls on us to "rejoice and be glad" (Matthew 5:12). But rather than being glad, many are ashamed of the gospel because it is so counter-cultural. Therefore, many compromise and reject the one, true, transcendent gospel. Jesus warns us that if salt loses its taste, it is useless.

Many in the culture today, by not preserving the gospel, have become tasteless salt and thus enemies of Christ. By undermining the gospel's transcendence in fear of men (rather than in fear of God), many well-intentioned Christians are doing more harm than good. When will Christians begin to take a stand for the gospel of Christ regardless of the cost? Jesus Himself was hated by His culture and yet we think that somehow we will not be? Christ calls for us to pick up our cross and follow Him (Matthew 10:38) and yet too many Christians today care more about survey's, opinion polls, cultural trends, and music styles than they do about the gospel.

The reason is because we do not value the gospel. If we truly valued the gospel, we would carefully preserve it. God must be ashamed of what we have become: cowards lacking boldness and "followers" lacking a cross.

To be conformed to the world is to invite heresy into our midst. When we spend more time debating the style of music in our worship or the dress code of our ministers than articulating the gospel to a lost world we miss the point. When our theology is determined more by the culture around us rather than by Scripture or the gospel, we become enemies of Christ. By our own conversations and debates, we show that we are more concerned with the will of men rather than the will of God. Such an approach only dilutes the gospel, robbing it of its saving power. To seek the culture's approval is to ignore God's. The culture, as we have seen, wants nothing to do with sin or repentance but rather embraces its current state of depravity and calls it progress. We have no need for a savior to save us because in our mind, there is nothing wrong. There is no greater danger than for the Church to define salvation and church growth by the ways of the world. It is difficult to be light of the world when our shade is as dark as the night (Matthew 5:14–17) and it is impossible to be salt of the earth if we fail to preserve the gospel entrusted to us (Matthew 5:13).

But this does not mean that we run from the world or try to escape the culture. To do so undermines the gospel and ignores our call to be ambassadors of Christ (2 Corinthians 5:20). We must, instead, be transcendent. God is not limited nor afraid of the culture for the gospel transcends all time and trends. If God is immutable, then His gospel is unshakable. Christians must be about the business of preaching and living out the transcendent gospel, not about chasing after the wind seeking cultural applause. By conforming to the culture, the gospel becomes diluted and no gospel at all. By fleeing from the culture, the gospel becomes secretive and limited to a selective few. The Christian worldview must accept neither option, but must rather proclaim a transcendent gospel that is undiluted and unfettered by the culture that boldly calls on men, everywhere, to repent.

Christians today are tempted to compromise such a gospel. In order to be better received by society, many have compromised their faith. Their reason is respectable, but the outcome is appalling. To compromise the gospel, along with its many social ramifications of repentance, is to trample on the cross of Jesus Christ. Christians must be willing to proclaim a hostile message of repentance in a Post-Christian world. Issues like sin, abortion, eugenics, homosexuality, sex, marriage, theology, family, the church, missions, ministry, salvation, secularism, law, politics, Scripture, and repentance are not mere issues of debates among academics and amateur theologians, but are gospel issues. Christians who refuse to defend life disregard the cross. Those who refuse to defend marriage miss the meaning of being the Bride of Christ. Those who lack discernment in politics and social debate do not understand sin and human nature.

To remain passive is to proclaim a corrupt gospel, especially when armed with the transcendent gospel. Caring more about our popularity than the destiny of man's souls or caring more about our perception within the culture than God's glory in saving sinners runs contrary to the gospel message and Biblical revelation. As Christians, we must be willing to forsake all for the glory of God and the proclamation of His Kingdom.

The Church must grow up. Rather than play dress up and mimic the culture, it is time for the Church to have a more consistent and articulate worldview, rooted in Scripture, and empowered by the Spirit. The gospel is not limited by cultural challenges or depravity, but transcends all that we face and fear. We live in a world more desperate for the gospel than ever before. Will we shout from the rooftops the glorious gospel of Jesus Christ, or will we continue to cower in the dark out of fear of hurting someone's feelings?

Christians have become lazy in understanding their worldview. This book has sought to help Christians, rooted in Scripture and powered by the gospel, to better understand their faith in order to more clearly articulate the gospel as they faithfully share the good news of Jesus Christ. The challenges we face are difficult, but not daunting. Through the power of the Spirit and His gospel, the Church can rise out of the cess pool of postmodernity stronger and more ready to "contend earnestly for the faith which was once for all handed down to the saints (Jude 3)."

Will we accept the call and rise to the challenge or be like Peter in the courtyard and cowardly proclaim, "I do not know the man" (Matthew 26:72, 74)? How precious and how valuable is the gospel to each of us? They will know we are Christians by the taste of our salt.

Bibliography

D'Souza, Dinesh. *Letters To a Young Conservative.* Jackson, TN: Basic, 2002.
——. *What's So Great About Christianity?* Washington, DC: Regnery, 2007.
Freud, Sigmund. *The Future of an Illusion.* New York: Norton, 1989.
Lewis, Clive Stables. *Mere Christianity.* San Francisco: Harper Collins, 2001.
Limbaugh, David. *Persecution: How Liberals Are Waging War Against Christians.* Washington, D. C.: Regnery, 2003.
McGrath, Alister. *The Twilight of Atheism: The Rise and Fall of Disbelief in the Modern World.* New York: Double Day, 2004.
Meacham, John. *The American Gospel: God, the Founding Fathers, and the Making of a Nation.* New York: Random House, 2006.
Mohler, R. Albert. *The Disappearance of God: Dangerous Beliefs in the New Spiritual Openness.* New York: Random House, 2009.
Schweikart, Larry and Michael Allen. *A Patriot's History of the United States: From Columbus's Great Discovery to the War on Terror.* New York: Penguin, 2004.
Singer, Peter. *Practical Ethics.* New York: Cambridge University Press, 1979.
Wallis, Jim. *The Great Awakening: Reviving Faith & Politics in a Post-Religious Right America.* New York: Harper Collins, 2008.

Internet Documentation

"A Social Creed for the 21st Century." No pages. Online: http://www.ncccusa.org/NCCdocs/A%20Social%20Creed%20for%20the%2021st%20Century.pdf.
Abrams, Joseph. "Little Rock Shooting Suspect Joins Growing List of Muslim Converts Accused of Targeting U.S." No pages. Online: http://www.foxnews.com/story/0,2933,524799,00.html.
Allen, Bob. "Rick Warren Says He Did Not Campaign For Proposition 8." No pages. Online: http://www.abpnews.com/index.php?option=com_content&task=view&id=3989&Itemid=53.
Allen, Charlotte. "Liberal Christianity is Paying for its Sins." No pages. Online: http://articles.latimes.com/2006/jul/09/opinion/op-allen9.

Bibliography

"Angry Parents Suing California Schools Over Mandatory Gay-Friendly Classes." No pages. Online: http://www.foxnews.com/story/0,2933,546280,00.html.

Aravosis, John. "President Obama Betrays the Gay Community: We Supported You. Time To Lie Up to Your Promises." No page. Online: http://www.salon.com/opinion/feature/2009/06/17/gay_rights/index.html.

Associated Press. "PETA Wishes Obama Hadn't Swatted that Fly." No pages. Online: http://www.huffingtonpost.com/2009/06/17/peta-wishes-obama-hadnt-s_n_217162.html.

Bailey, Sarah Pulliam. "Pat Robertson: Haiti 'Cursed' Since Pact with the Devil." No pages. Online: http://blog.christianitytoday.com/ctliveblog/archives/2010/01/pat_robertson_h.html.

Barnett, Lindsay. "PETA Wants to Replace Famous Groundhog Punxsutawney Phil with an Animatronic Replica." No pages. Online: http://latimesblogs.latimes.com/unleashed/2010/01/animatronic-punxsutawney-phil-peta-groundhog-day.html.

Bazelon, Emily. "The Place of Women on the Court." *New York Times*. 4 Pages. Online: http://www.nytimes.com/2009/07/12/magazine/12ginsburg-t.html?pagewanted=4.

Brown, Jim. "Rick Warren Disavows Support for Proposition 8," No pages. Online: http://www.onenewsnow.com/Culture/Default.aspx?id=481280.

Burk, Denny. "A Second Tornado in Minneapolis." No pages. Online: http://www.dennyburk.com/?p=5069.

Burkhardt, Gail. "Crystal Dixon Sues UT for Rights Violation." No pages. Online: http://www.toledofreepress.com/2008/12/05/crystal-dixon-sues-ut-for-rights-violations/.

Byrd, A. Dean. "'Homosexuality Is Not Hardwired,' Concludes Head of Human Genome Project." No page. Online: http://www.lifesitenews.com/ldn/2007/mar/07032003.htm.

Capuzzo, Jill P. "Group Loses Tax Break Over Gay Union Issue." No page. Online: http://www.nytimes.com/2007/09/18/nyregion/18grove.html.

Cleveland, Adam Walker. "John Piper Contributes to Culture of Fear." No pages. Online: http://pomomusings.com/2009/08/20/john-piper/.

Cohen, Randy. "Open the Marriage, Close the Door." No pages. Online: http://www.nytimes.com/2010/01/31/magazine/31FOB-ethicist-t.html.

Colson, Charles. "The Coming Persecution: How Same-Sex 'Marriage' Will Harm Christians." No pages. Online: http://www.christianpost.com/article/20080702/the-coming-persecution/index.html.

Corsey, Shane. "God, Conservatism, and Values." No page. Online: http://www.americanthinker.com/2009/10/god_conservatism_and_values.html.

Bibliography

Dixon, Crystal. "Gay Rights and Wrongs: Another Perspective." No pages. Online: http://www.toledofreepress.com/2008/04/18/gay-rights-and-wrongs-another-perspective/.

"Encore Presentation: Interview With Joel Osteen. No pages. Online: http://transcripts.cnn.com/TRANSCRIPTS/0507/03/lkl.01.html.

Gilbert, Kathleen. "Team of Researchers Blames Children's Films for Perpetuating 'Heteronormativity.'" No page. Online: http://www.lifesitenews.com/ldn/2009/jun/09062404.html.

Gilgoff, Dan. "Rick Warren: Stopping Gay Marriage 'Very Low' on Priority List." No pages. Online: http://www.usnews.com/blogs/god-and-country/2009/04/07/rick-warren-stopping-gay-marriage-very-low-on-priority-list.html.

Gillette, Felix. "Primary Scream." No pages. Online: http://www.observer.com/2008/primary-scream?page=0%2C0.

Graham, Don. "From Cross to Crescent: Islam Triples in Europe." 3 pages. Online: http://www.crosswalk.com/11594618/page0/.

Grant, Tobin. *Glenn Beck: 'Leave Your Church.'* 4 pages. Online: http://www.christianitytoday.com/ct/2010/marchweb-only/20-51.0.html.

Guttmacher Institute. "Facts on Induced Abortion in the United States." No pages. Online: http://www.guttmacher.org/pubs/fb_induced_abortion.html.

Hechtkopf, Kevin. "Humans on Display at London's Zoo," 2 Pages. Online: http://www.cbsnews.com/stories/2005/08/26/world/main798423.shtml.

Hoffman, Matthew Cullinan. "Christian Prayer Group Sexually and Physically Assualted by Homsoexual Mob: San Francisco Castro Distric Residents Seek Vengeance for Vote on Proposition 8." No pages. Online: http://www.lifesitenews.com/ldn/2008/nov/08111816.html.

Jalsevac, John. "Homosexualist Anarchists Storm Michigan Church During Sunday Service." No pages. Online: http://www.lifesitenews.com/ldn/2008/nov/08111104.html.

Jayson, Sharon. "Sooner vs. Later: Is there an Ideal Age for First Marriage?" No pages. Online: http://www.usatoday.com/news/health/2008-11-09-delayed-marriage_N.htm.

Jha, Alok. "Global Warming: Blame the Forests." No page. Online: http://www.guardian.co.uk/science/2006/jan/12/environment.climatechange.

Jones, Tony. "Who Will Call Out John Piper?" No pages. Online: http://blog.beliefnet.com/tonyjones/2009/08/who-will-call-out-john-piper.html.

"Kennedy's Letter to the Pope." No page. Online: http://www.washingtonpost.com/wp-dyn/content/article/2009/08/29/AR2009082902702.html.

Lean, Geoffrey. "Cow 'Emissions' More Damaging to Planet Than CO2 Cars." No page. Online: http://www.independent.co.uk/environment/climate

Bibliography

-change/cow-emissions-more-damaging-to-planet-than-cosub2sub-from-cars-427843.html.

MacArthur, John. "The Christian's Responsibility to Government—Part 1," No pages. Online: http://www.biblebb.com/files/mac/sg45-97.htm.

Mattews, Chris. "'Hardball with Christ Matthews' for Friday, Jude 5." No pages. Online: http://www.msnbc.msn.com/id/31173133.

Mintz, Evan. "Lakewood: All the Fire Without the Brimstone." No pages. Online: http://the.ricethresher.org/opinion/2005/10/07/lakewood_church.

Mohler, R. Albert. "A Christian Vision of Beauty, Part 3." No pages. Online: http://www.albertmohler.com/2005/11/18/a-christian-vision-of-beauty-part-three/.

———. "A New Search and Destroy Mission," No pages. Online: http://www.albertmohler.com/2008/07/01/a-new-search-and-destroy-mission/.

———. "Europeans Awakening to the Islamic Threat?" No pages. Online: http://www.albertmohler.com/blog_read.php?id=789.

———. "Polyamory—The Perfectly Plural Postmodern Condition." No page. Online: http://www.albertmohler.com/blog_read.php?id=4211.

———. "'Pressure to Keep the Baby?' – The Descent Continues." No pages. Online: http://www.albertmohler.com/2008/09/15/pressure-to-keep-the-baby-the-descent-continues/.

———. "Will Babies With Down Syndrome Just Disappear?" No pages. Online: http://www.albertmohler.com/2009/09/18/will-babies-with-down-syndrome-just-disappear/.

Morford, Mark. "God Does Not Want 16 Kids: Arkansas Mom Gives Birth to a Whole Freakin' Baseball Team. How Deeply Should You Cringe?" No pages. Online: http://www.sfgate.com/cgi-bin/article.cgi?file=/gate/archive/2005/10/19/notes101905.DTL.

Obama, Barack. "Remarks by the President in the State of the Union Address." No pages. Online: http://www.whitehouse.gov/the-press-office/remarks-president-state-union-address.

Paris, Jenell Williams. "The Toddler, the Discharge, and The Humidity." No pages. Online: http://jenellparis.blogspot.com/2009/08/toddler-discharge-and-humidity-john.html.

Pawlowski, A. "Mate Debate: Is Monogamy Realistic?" No pages. Online: http://www.cnn.com/2009/LIVING/10/28/monogamy.realistic.today/index.html.

PETA. "The Breast is Best! PETA Asks Ben & Jerry's to Dump Dairy and Go With Human Milk Instead." No pages. Online: http://www.peta.org/mc/NewsItem.asp?id=11993.

Bibliography

Piazza, Joe. "Audience Experiences 'Avatar Blues.'" No pages. Online: http://www.cnn.com/2010/SHOWBIZ/Movies/01/11/avatar.movie.blues/index.html.

Piper, John. "Clarifying the Tornado." No pages. Online: http://www.desiringgod.org/Blog/1968_clarifying_the_tornado.

———. "The Tornado, the Lutherans, and Homosexuality." No pages. Online: http://www.desiringgod.org/Blog/1965_the_tornado_the_lutherans_and_homosexuality/.

"Robertson: God May Smite Down Town That Voted Out Anti-Evolution School Board," No pages. Online: http://www.foxnews.com/story/0,2933,175247,00.html.

Robinson, Jeff. "Mohler: 80-90% of Down Syndrome Babies Killed in Push for 'Human Perfection,'" No pages. Online: http://www.bpnews.net/BPnews.asp?ID=22533.

Romans, Christine. "Can Joel Osteen Help You Pay Your Bills?" No pages. Online: http://www.cnn.com/2009/US/12/18/romans.osteen/index.html.

Singer, Peter. "Heavy Petting." No pages. Online: http://www.nerve.com/Opinions/Singer/heavyPetting/main.asp.

Singh, Madhur. "Cows with Gas: India's Global Warming Problem." No pages. Online: http://www.time.com/time/world/article/0,8599,1890646,00.html.

Shaw, Liz. "Former Co-Worker Describes Dead Anti-Abortion Activist, Killed Friday Morning in From of Owosso High School, as Radical and Committed." No pages. Online: http://www.mlive.com/news/flint/index.ssf/2009/09/former_coworker_describes_dead.html.

———. "Homicide Victim James Pouillon Had Extensive Background of Civil Violations, Many Related to Anti-Abortion Protest." No pages. Online: http://www.mlive.com/news/flint/index.ssf/2009/09/homicide_victim_james_pouillon.html.

Tatchell, Peter. "Homosexuality: It Isn't Natural." No pages. Online: http://www.spiked-online.com/index.php?/site/article/5375/.

Tatusko, Drew. "The Tornado to Stop the "Gays." No pages. Online: http://notes-from-offcenter.com/2009/08/20/the-tornado-to-stop-the-gays/.

"The Human Zoo." No pages. Online: http://www.zsl.org/print/zsl-london-zoo/news/the-human-zoo,180,NS.html.

Thomas, Evan. "The Perils of Punditry: How Bloggers Turned Me into the Poster Child for the Argument that the Liberal Press Loves Obama." No pages. Online: http://www.newsweek.com/id/202010.

Toner, Robin. "Democrats Attack Bush on Women's Health Issues." No pages. Online: http://www.nytimes.com/2007/07/18/us/politics/18abort.html?fta=y.

Tuhus-Dubrow, Rebecca. "I Now Pronounce You . . . Friend and Friend: Some Argue It's Time to Legally Recognize the Bond of Friendship." 4 pages.

Bibliography

Online: http://www.boston.com/bostonglobe/ideas/articles/2008/06/08/i_now_pronounce_you____friend_and_friend/.

Wallis, Jim. "A New Conversation on Abortion." No pages. Online: http://blog.sojo.net/2008/10/16/a-new-conversation-on-abortion/.

———. "Tell Glenn Beck: I'm a Social Justice Christian." No pages. Online: http://blog.sojo.net/2010/03/10/tell-glenn-beck-im-a-social-justice-christian/.

Weddington, Ron. "Weddington to Clinton," No pages. Online: http://www.lifesitenews.com/ldn/2006_docs/WeddingtontoClintondocs.pdf.

Wen, Patricia. "Catholic Charities Stuns State, Ends Adoptions." No pages. Online: http://www.boston.com/news/local/articles/2006/03/11/catholic_charities_stuns_state_ends_adoptions/.

Yount, Blake. "Hate Crimes Bill Will Not Provide Equality Before the Law According to US Attorney General." No pages. Online: http://www.examiner.com/x-13430-Sarpy-County-Conservative-Examiner~y2009m7d3-Hate-crimes-bill-will-not-provide-equality-before-the-law-according-to-US-Attorney-General.

www.ingramcontent.com/pod-product-compliance
Lightning Source LLC
Chambersburg PA
CBHW072140160426
43197CB00012B/2185